HOW TO RAISE A MILLIONAIRE: FINANCIAL STRATEGIES FOR YOUR KIDS. HOW TO FOSTER A MILLIONAIRE MINDSET IN TODAY'S GENERATION OF KIDS.

Adam Diesel

BUSINESS BOOKS

Copyright © 2023 Adam Diesel

All rights reserved

The characters and events portrayed in this book are fictitious. Any similarity to real persons, living or dead, is coincidental and not intended by the author.

No part of this book may be reproduced, or stored in a retrieval system, or transmitted in any form or by any means, electronic, mechanical, photocopying, recording, or otherwise, without express written permission of the publisher.

Cover design by: Art Painter
Library of Congress Control Number: 2018675309
Printed in the United States of America

I Want to thank you and congratulate you for buying my book
How to Raise a Millionaire: Financial Strategies for Your Kids. How to Foster a Millionaire Mindset in Today's Generation of Kids.

Millionaire kids

Millionaire kids can be successful by developing a combination of habits and knowledge. It is important to cultivate a healthy mindset that will help support their success. Some of the habits that millionaire kids should practice include setting goals, saving money, making wise investments, working hard, learning new skills, networking with influential people, and taking calculated risks. Additionally, they should acquire knowledge in a variety of areas, including finance, accounting, economics, marketing, and business. By developing these habits and knowledge, millionaire kids can build a strong foundation for success. With dedication and hard work, they have the potential to become millionaires in little time.

In addition to the habits and knowledge mentioned above, millionaire kids need to have a clear understanding of their finances. This includes developing a budget, tracking expenses, and identifying areas where they can save. Being mindful of their spending habits can help them allocate resources in the most efficient way possible. It is also important to ensure that investments are researched thoroughly, as well as diversified across different asset classes. If done correctly, these investments can help build a substantial amount of wealth over time.

Millionaire kids should strive to stay motivated and focused on their goals. They should also take advantage of every opportunity that comes their way and always look for ways to improve themselves. With the right combination of habits and knowledge, they have the potential to become successful millionaires in no time.

With the right combination of habits and knowledge, millionaire kids can cultivate success for themselves and work towards becoming wealthy. Through building discipline, staying determined, and understanding financial decisions, they can achieve their dreams of becoming millionaires. With dedication and hard work, they have the potential to become successful millionaires in no time.

CHAPTER 1: IMPORTANCE OF CULTIVATING STRONG FINANCIAL HABITS EARLY IN CHILDHOOD

Financial literacy is an important skill to have throughout our lives, but it's especially important to cultivate strong financial habits from a young age. Financial habits can set kids up for success in their adult life and help them become millionaires one day.

Here Are Some :

1. How to Learn the Value of Money?

If you want to help your kids become millionaires, it's important for them to learn the value of money. Teaching your children about money can be a difficult task, but there are a few simple tips that can help get them started:

1. Explain How Money Works: Start by teaching your children the basics about how money works. Explain to them the concept of budgeting, saving and investing.

2. Help Them Set Goals: Once you have taught your children about money, help them set goals for how they want to use it. This could be something as simple as setting aside money each month for an allowance or a big-ticket item like a car or a house.

3. Create an Allowance System: Give your children an allowance each month to help teach them the

value of money. Explain that it's important to save some and spend some in order to be able to afford what they want in the future.

4. Teach Them How To Save: Encourage your kids to save a portion of their allowance each month. Explain the importance of setting aside money for the future and show them how even small amounts can add up over time.

5. Help Them Invest Wisely: If your kids have extra money, suggest that they consider investing it in stocks or mutual funds. Teach them about different types of investments and help them choose the ones that make the most sense for their financial goals.

A-Have Early Conversations About Money Together

Parents need to have early conversations with their children about money if they want them to become millionaires. Money isn't just something that magically materializes in the bank; it is earned, saved and invested. Teaching your kids these concepts from a young age will help them understand why you make certain decisions or can't buy them everything they want.

The most important thing to teach your kids about money is that it is not a given. You must work hard and make smart decisions in order to accumulate wealth. Explain the concept of budgeting, saving for long-term goals and investing in stocks and other financial products. Make sure they understand that these decisions have an impact on their future and that the results will be determined by their own actions.

Helping your children understand the basics of personal finance is key for them to become millionaires. Showing them how to think long-term and save up for bigger purchases can help instil a sense of frugality and responsibility when it comes to money. It also teaches them the importance of investing in their future.

Explain to your kids that millionaires don't become rich overnight and that it requires planning and hard work. Let them know that becoming a millionaire isn't easy, but it's certainly achievable with dedication and perseverance. Encourage them to start thinking about ways they can make smart financial decisions that will help them get there.

B-How To Help Them Set Goals?

When it comes to helping kids become millionaires, the first step is to help them set goals. Goal setting can be a powerful tool in helping children achieve their dreams of becoming successful entrepreneurs. To start, encourage your child to think about what they want to accomplish and how they will go about achieving it. Ask them questions such as: What do they want to accomplish? What strategies do they plan on using to reach their goals? What steps will they need to take in order to get there?

Once your child has developed some goals, help them create a timeline for reaching those targets. This timeline should include milestones that can be used as stepping stones towards the big goal. For example, if the ultimate goal is to become a millionaire, you may want to create mini-goals such as launching a business or increasing your investment portfolio.

It's also important to ensure that your child's goals are realistic and attainable. Help them break down their goals into manageable chunks so that they don't get overwhelmed by the process. If the goal seems too big or intimidating, it may be best to break it down into smaller items that can be completed over time.

Once your child has set their goals and created a timeline for achieving them, provide ongoing support and encouragement. This could include talking with them about progress updates, helping them stay motivated and providing resources that can help make their goals attainable.

C-How To Create An Allowance System?

Creating an allowance system for your children is a great way to teach them about personal finance. It allows them to learn how to manage their money, budget it out and makes them more responsible. Here are the steps you'll need to create an effective allowance system:

1. Decide on a policy - Before setting up an allowance

system, you'll need to decide on an appropriate policy for how much money your child will receive. Consider their age and what expenses they may need help with, such as clothing or school supplies.

2. Set up a budget - Once you have decided on the amount of money to give your kid each month, create a budget that outlines all of their expected expenses. This will help them understand how to budget and prioritize spending.

3. Be consistent - Consistency is key when it comes to teaching your child about money management. Make sure you stick to the same allowance for each month, and stay on top of any discrepancies or overspending.

4. Encourage saving - Encourage your child to save a portion of their allowance each month. This will help them develop good habits and become more responsible with money.

5. Reward progress - When your kid meets their financial goals, reward it with something special that they can look forward to. It could be a small treat or toy, but it's important to incentivize their progress.

D-How To Teach Them How To Save?

Teaching children to save can be challenging, but it's an essential skill for success. Here are some tips for teaching your kids how to save:

1. Start young. Teaching children the importance of saving is most effective when they are young. Helping them learn how to count money and set goals for their savings can help them develop strong savings habits.
2. Set goals. It's important to encourage children to set both short-term and long-term goals for their savings. Helping them understand why it is important to save and how saving now can help them achieve their future dreams will motivate them to keep up the habit of saving.
3. Open a savings account. Opening a savings account for your child is a great way to start building their financial literacy and encourage them to save. There are different types of savings accounts available, so be sure to do your research and find one that will best suit your child's needs and goals.
4. Make saving fun. Encouraging your children to save can be made more enjoyable by turning it into a game or challenge. You can have your child set up a savings jar and try to fill it with an agreed-upon amount each month or you could give them challenges like saving the money they get from birthdays and holidays.
5. Talk about money. Discussing finances with your children is an important part of teaching them how to save and manage their money in the future. Take the time to explain concepts like budgeting, taxes, and investing to give your kids a better understanding of how saving works.

2. Developing Smart Spending Habits

One of the best ways to become a successful millionaire as a kid is by developing smart spending habits. Here are some tips and strategies for teaching children to make wise financial decisions:
A. Teach kids the importance of delayed gratification
B. Teach kids to save
C. Give teens financial freedom

A. How To Teach Kids The Importance Of Delayed Gratification?

Teaching kids the importance of delayed gratification is an important step in helping them become financially successful. The concept can be difficult to explain and understand, but there are a few key strategies that parents can use to help children understand the value of waiting for rewards or gratification.

One way to demonstrate the idea of delayed gratification is by setting up a budget and savings plan for the family. Parents can explain to their children that spending too much money now reduces the amount they have available in the future. Showing kids how setting aside even small amounts of money each month can add up over time to help with long-term goals is a great way to reinforce this concept.

Another way to help teach the importance of

delayed gratification is to talk about investments and how they can work for them in the long term. Showing kids how investing in stocks, mutual funds, or other assets can grow over time with careful planning helps demonstrate that patience and waiting now can pay off down the road.

Encouraging children to set short and long-term goals and rewards can also help them understand the value of delayed gratification. For example, if a child wants to buy a new console game, parents can explain how setting aside money for that purchase over time is better than buying it all at once. This helps teach kids that patience now will allow them to get what they want in the future.

Parents should be good role models and practice what they preach. Showing children how to budget, save, invest, and set goals can help make the concept of delayed gratification more real for them. Kids will learn better from seeing their parents actually doing these things than just hearing about them in theory.

B. What Are The Steps To Teach Kids To Save?

1. Make it fun: Include children in financial discussions and encourage them to come up with ideas that will help them save money. Try turning saving into a game or reward system, so they can see the positive side of not spending their money frivolously.

2. Teach by example: Set an example for your children by practising good saving habits yourself. Show them how you save money and talk about

strategies that have worked for you.

3. Give an allowance: Providing a set sum of money to children each month allows them to understand the concept of budgeting and managing their own funds without relying on parents or guardians for extra spending money. This is a great way to teach them the value of money.

4. Open up a savings account: Take your child to the bank and open up a savings account in their name to help foster an understanding of saving, as well as encourage them to save regularly. Even small amounts will add up over time, which is a great lesson for kids to learn.

5. Offer incentives: Offering incentives for good savings habits is a great way to get kids excited about saving money. Set up a reward system where they can receive a prize or treat if they reach certain saving goals. This will help reinforce the idea that saving money is rewarding and should be done consistently.

C. Give Teens Financial Freedom

The best way to give teens financial freedom is to teach them the basics of money management, provide guidance and support, and help them develop a budget.

Start by teaching teens about the importance of saving. Explain how they can use money for short-term goals such as buying clothes or going on trips, while also setting aside some for the future. Show them how to set up an emergency fund and help them create a budget that includes their basic necessities such as food, rent, and utilities.

Once teens understand the basics of money management, it's important to give them some freedom. Encourage them to make decisions about spending their own money, such as what to buy or how much to save. Set clear boundaries, and if they make mistakes, help them learn from them rather than punishing them.

When teens are ready for more responsibility, consider giving them a credit card with a low limit. This is a great way to teach teens how to handle credit responsibly and avoid debt. Be sure to talk to them about how credit works and what could happen if they misuse it.

Provide guidance and support when teens make financial decisions. Don't just tell them what to do; guide them through the process of making financial decisions. This will help them learn more about managing their money and give them a greater sense of responsibility.

3. Building Financial Confidence

This is a great question for parents who want to help their kids become millionaires. Financial confidence is essential to achieving any financial goal, and it's especially important for young people who are just starting out in the world of money management. Here are some tips for helping kids build financial confidence:

1. Talk about money openly - Having open, honest

conversations about money with your kids is key for helping them understand finances and build financial confidence. Discuss topics like budgeting, compound interest, investment strategies, and the importance of saving.

2. Set a good example - Kids often learn more by watching than they do from what we tell them. Be sure to set a good example by living within your means, avoiding debt, and saving regularly.

3. Give them small responsibilities - Assigning your kids tasks such as tracking their spending or helping to research financial products will give them a sense of responsibility and help instil the knowledge they need to make good financial decisions.

4. Teach them how to shop smart - Show your children how to comparison shop and look for deals. This will not only help them become more savvy buyers but also give them the confidence they need when making purchases.

5. Have patience - Building financial confidence takes time, and it's important to remember that kids learn at their own pace. As long as you stay patient and encouraging, your children will become more confident with their finances over time.

These tips for helping kids build financial confidence provide a great starting point, but you may need to adjust them depending on the unique needs of your children. Whether you're teaching basic budgeting skills or more complex concepts like investing, your kids must be able to gain a sense of confidence in their own abilities. With the right guidance and support, your children can become the millionaires you know they deserve to be!

4. Avoiding Costly Mistakes

Young millionaires can easily fall into the trap of making costly mistakes with their newfound wealth. Here are some tips on how to avoid these costly missteps:

1. Don't get caught up in the flashy lifestyle. Many young people think that as soon as they have money, they should start living a lavish lifestyle. However, this can be a fast way to blow through your money quickly. One way to avoid this is by setting clear financial goals for yourself and sticking to them.

2. Don't put all your eggs in one basket. Just like with any other type of investment, it's important to diversify your assets so that you're not putting all your eggs in one basket. This means investing some of your money in stocks, bonds, real estate, or other types of investments to help reduce the risk of a total loss.

3. Don't get caught up in risky investments. Be careful when it comes to high-risk investments such as penny stocks, cryptocurrency, or leveraged trading. These types of investments can lead to huge losses if you're not careful.

4. Don't forget about taxes. When it comes to investing and earning money, taxes are a reality that must be taken into account. Setting aside some of your earnings for taxes each year can help you avoid getting in trouble with the IRS.

Savings And Budgeting

Savings and budgeting are two of the most important skills needed to become a millionaire. Teaching your children early how to save and budget their money will give them a head start on learning financial responsibility.

Encouraging your child to set financial goals is an essential part of their journey to becoming a millionaire. Setting these goals will help build motivation to achieve the desired outcome. Make sure these goals are achievable and within reach of your child's capabilities.

Teach your child the basics of budgeting by creating a monthly spending plan. This will help them understand how to allocate their money into different categories such as savings, entertainment, bills and other expenses. Encourage your child to track their spending habits to ensure they are staying on track with their budget.

Saving money is also a key part of becoming a millionaire. Help your child develop good saving habits by setting aside small amounts of money each week or month and encourage them to open a savings account. Show your child how their savings can grow exponentially over time through the power of compound interest.

These lessons are the foundation for creating a successful financial life and will help them work towards their goal of becoming a millionaire. By teaching your child the basics of savings and budgeting, you will be setting them up to reach their financial goals.

How To Set Your Kid Up To Become A Millionaire

One of the best gifts you can give your child is to set them up for financial success. Teaching your kid how to become a millionaire will not only help them build wealth, but also give them the confidence and skills to manage their finances in a responsible way. Here are some tips on how to set your kid up for long-term financial success:

1. Start Teaching Early – It's never too early to start teaching your child about money and finances. This could range from basic concepts such as the difference between saving and spending, or more advanced topics like how to make a budget or invest wisely.

2. Talk About Goals – Explain to your kid why it's important to save money and set financial goals. Encourage your child to dream big and come up with attainable objectives that can help them achieve their long-term financial dreams.

3. Get Them a Savings Account – Open a savings account for your kid as early as possible, so they can start building up their wealth from an early age.

4. Make Investments – Consider investing in stocks, mutual funds, or other assets to help your kid build wealth over time.

5. Encourage Entrepreneurship – Encourage your child to explore their entrepreneurial side by starting a business or launching a website that can

generate income over time.

6. Be a Role Model – One of the best ways to ensure your kid's long-term financial success is to lead by example. Show them how you handle money responsibly and discuss strategies that have worked for you in the past.

7. Teach the Power of Compounding Interest – Explain to your child that their money can work for them by earning compounding interest. Even small amounts of money invested early in life can grow significantly over time due to the power of compound interest.

8. Show Them How to Spend Wisely – Teach your kid about the importance of spending smart and living within their means.

9. Have Fun With Finances – Make learning about finances a fun activity. You can play board games together that help them learn concepts such as budgeting and saving, or find online resources that make learning about money enjoyable for your kid.

10. Keep a Positive Mindset – Above all, remind your kid that they are capable of achieving financial success and encourage them to stay focused on their goals.

CHAPTER 2: KID MILLIONAIRES
AGE 6 TO 8

Ages Six to Eight is a great age to start teaching kids about money and how to become millionaires. There are several ways parents can help guide their children towards financial success:

1. Introduce budgeting concepts – Talk to your child about budgeting, emphasizing the importance of sticking with it. Show them how having a plan allows them to save for important things, like college, a car, or a home.

2. Teach them the value of delayed gratification – Explain to your child that not all purchases need to be made immediately. Show them how waiting and saving up for something can be far more rewarding than just buying it at the spur of the moment.

3. Introduce the School of Hard Knocks – Explain to your child that sometimes life throws you a curveball and you need to adjust your budget. Show them how to create an emergency fund, save for big purchases, and manage unexpected expenses.

4. Set up a savings account – Open a savings account for your child so he or she can watch their money grow. This will help your child understand the basics of saving and can provide an incentive for them to reach their financial goals.

5. Start investing – Teach your child about

investments and why it's important to diversify their portfolio. Show them how stocks, bonds, mutual funds, and other types of investments can help build wealth.

Consistency In Every Aspect Of Life

Consistency in Every Aspect of Life is key to developing the millionaire mindset. This means that children should be given the same opportunities at home and in school so they can develop a strong work ethic and attitude. Parents need to be consistent with rules, discipline, and rewards to ensure that their children understand the importance of hard work. Additionally, parents should encourage their children to participate in activities such as sports, arts and music to further develop their skills. It is also important to involve the children in family conversations about finances so they understand the importance of budgeting and saving for a rainy day. Finally, make sure that your child has access to materials such as books and other resources to help them stay informed about money management strategies. With these practices in place, children will be better prepared to become millionaires when they reach adulthood.

By setting a good example and establishing consistent habits, you can give your kids the tools they need to become a millionaire in the future. Encourage them to practice skills such as budgeting and saving early on and teach them how to make smart financial decisions. Show them how their hard work can pay off and instil in them the value of investing in themselves instead of wasting money on frivolous items.

Emphasizing The Importance Of Teamwork

Emphasizing the Importance of Teamwork is one of the key ways to help millionaire kids ages six to eight reach their potential. As they grow and develop, they need to understand that everyone has something valuable to contribute and that working together can lead to greater success than trying to do everything alone. Encourage children in this age group to work together on activities such as group projects, games, and sports. Talk about the importance of positive collaboration and helping each other out when needed. Show them examples of successful teams that have worked hard to reach their goals, such as athletes, business leaders, or even a family working together towards a common goal. By emphasizing the importance of teamwork early on in life, kids will be better equipped to reach their goals later in life.

Additionally, it may be beneficial for kids in this age group to practice team-building activities. These can help them gain a better understanding of how teams work and what it takes to make a successful team. Encourage them to brainstorm ideas together and come up with plans on how they will tackle tasks or solve problems. Through these activities, kids will be able to appreciate the value of collaboration and learn how to work together effectively.

By emphasizing the importance of teamwork in kids ages six to eight, they can develop invaluable skills that will help them as they grow and reach their goals. Parents and mentors need to provide guidance and support that will help kids understand the power of working together. Through team-building activities, communication, and collaboration, kids can take their first steps towards becoming millionaires.

Recognizing The Value Of Leadership

Recognizing the Value of Leadership is a great starting point for millionaire kids ages six to eight. Leadership teaches children how to be confident in their skills, set and enforce goals, make decisions, and develop problem-solving skills. Encourage your child to speak up in group settings and take the lead on activities. Point out strong leadership examples from people they admire such as their teachers, parents, and peers. Encourage them to read books focusing on strong leaders or have them watch videos of successful influential people to further understand the power of leadership.

Leadership skills can be taught through activities such as planning a family picnic or trip; setting kitchen rules and helping enforce them; making grocery lists for trips to the store; many more. Allowing your child to take the lead in these activities will help them recognize their ability to make decisions and show leadership. Teaching children the value of leadership at a young age can prepare them for success as millionaires later in life. You can also provide other resources such as books on saving and investing money, showing them how to budget, and introducing the idea of starting a business. Having these skills early will help them understand how to properly manage their money as they grow older. Your child must understand the power of leadership and money management before age eight if you want them to be successful millionaires in the future.

When children are given the opportunity to take the lead and recognize their own leadership capabilities, they become more confident in themselves and have a better understanding of what it takes to be successful. Showing your child how to value leadership is a great way to set them up for success from a young age.

Engaging In Money-Related Games With Your Kids

Engaging in Money-Related Games with Your Kids is a great way to teach kids about money. There are plenty of fun and educational games available that can help your children learn the basics of budgeting, saving, and investing. Board games like Monopoly, Cashflow 101, The Game of Life, and Stock Market Challenge are all excellent options for teaching kids basic financial concepts. Additionally, there are many apps and online versions of these games available that can be used for free or with a minimal fee.

Playing money-related board games with your

kids can be an entertaining way to introduce them to the concept of investing, so they understand how it works. You can also use these games as opportunities to discuss strategies like diversifying investments and planning for the future. Additionally, having conversations about money and how best to use it can help your kids understand concepts like budgeting, saving, and spending wisely.

Finally, teaching kids to be mindful of their financial decisions is an important step in helping them become financially responsible adults. Encouraging them to make wise money choices can help them develop good habits that will stay with them for life. By engaging in money-related games, your kids can gain the knowledge and skills they need to become successful millionaires.

Establishing Family Financial Objectives

Establishing Family Financial Objectives is one of the most important steps to becoming a millionaire kid. Parents should guide their children in setting financial goals, such as saving money for college or helping pay off debt. Setting these objectives will help children develop an understanding of how finances work and give them a sense of responsibility and accountability when it comes to money management. Parents can also introduce budgeting tools such as spreadsheets and calculators to help kids understand where their money is going and how it can be handled more effectively. Additionally, teaching children about the importance of saving for retirement will show them that long-term objectives can also be achieved through smart money management. Establishing family financial objectives will help young millionaires learn fundamental skills that will set them up for success in the future.

In addition to setting family financial objectives, teaching kids about investing is also important for becoming a millionaire kid. Introducing concepts such as stocks, bonds, mutual funds and index funds can help children develop a basic understanding of how investments work and why they are an important part of achieving long-term wealth. Additionally, discussing the possible risks associated with investments can help children understand how to manage their money and minimize potential losses in the future. By taking the time to teach kids about investing, parents will be giving them an opportunity to create long-lasting wealth that will set them up for success in the future.

Teaching kids about financial responsibility is key to becoming a millionaire kid. Setting limits on spending and teaching kids how to identify needs versus wants will help children learn how to manage their money in the most effective way possible. Asking kids to keep track of their expenses can give them an understanding of where their money is going and what can be done to reduce unnecessary spending. Teaching kids about the importance of long-term planning and goal setting will also help them understand how to use their money in a responsible manner. By instilling these values into children, parents can give their kids the tools they need to become successful millionaires.

Overcoming The Lifestyle Habit

At a young age, many kids are stuck in lifestyle habits that are not conducive to wealth building. The good news is that parents can teach their children how to break these detrimental patterns and cultivate healthy financial habits early on.

One of the key steps for helping kids become millionaires is teaching them how to overcome lifestyle habits such as spending beyond their means, impulse buying, and constantly wanting the newest and most expensive toys or clothing.

Parents can do this by setting a good example for their kids, teaching them about budgeting and smart spending habits, and helping them understand not only how to spend money wisely but also why it is important to do so. A great way to do this is to give them an allowance and set up a reward system for responsible money management. Establishing an understanding of the value of a dollar from a young age and teaching kids the right way to spend and save their money can help them become millionaires in the future. Making sure that they are able to accumulate wealth by saving rather than spending will give them a great start on their path to becoming successful adults.

Creating A Joint Bank Account For You And Your Child

Creating a joint bank account for you and your child is a great way to teach them about money management and responsible spending. This also provides the opportunity to set up an allowance system, which encourages children to save money as well as use it responsibly. Depending on the age of your child, you can determine how much is in their account and what they can and cannot spend it on. For example, you may choose to put in a set amount each month or week and allow your child to use it for necessary items, such as school supplies or food. Setting rules regarding what they can buy and how much they need to save is important for teaching financial literacy. It also helps them become more aware of how much things cost and the value of money. Additionally, involving your child in these decisions can help them become more engaged with their account and learn important financial lessons. Having a joint bank account is also beneficial for teaching budgeting skills to your millionaire kid. You can show them how to divide up their allowance into different categories, such as saving, spending, and investing. This can help give them an early understanding of financial planning and the importance of budgeting for their future. It's also a great way to start teaching them the basics of investing and how to make wise decisions about their money.

The Power Of Interest To Work For Your Money

The Power of Interest to Work for Your Money is an important concept for kids aged six to eight to understand. Interest is something that will work for you and help you accumulate wealth. To show this, it might be beneficial to set up a simple piggy bank savings account with your child's name on it. By doing this, they can watch their money grow as they save more and more. When they see a higher balance they will be motivated to save more of their money as well as understand just how powerful interest rates can be.

It is also important to explain the concept of compound interest and how it works. Compound interest ensures that not only will your child receive the initial amount of money saved, but they will also receive interest on the interest earned. This is a powerful way for kids to realize that their money can grow exponentially if they continue to save and put their money in an account with a good interest rate.

Kids aged six to eight need to understand the power of Interest and how it can work for them when saving money. By setting up a simple piggy bank savings account and explaining both simple and compound interest to them, kids can begin their journey as millionaires!

Active And Passive Income

It's never too early for kids to start learning about the differences between active and passive income. Once they have a basic understanding of money, ages six to eight is an ideal time for parents to introduce the concept of income streams.

Active income is earned by working for a salary or wage. It is usually considered the most reliable form of income because it is a fixed amount determined by the hours or days worked. Examples include working a job, tutoring, teaching music lessons and so on.

Passive income involves making money from investments such as stocks, bonds, real estate and royalties from intellectual property. Passive income can take longer to realize than active income but can provide an ongoing source of income. Examples include real estate investing, stock trading and owning rental properties.

By helping kids to understand the different types of income, their natural curiosity can be ignited as they explore potential income opportunities. Parents must also emphasize the importance of budgeting responsibly so that children are able to develop healthy financial habits early on in life.

The key for millionaire kids is understanding that both active and passive income is necessary to build up wealth and become successful. Explaining the differences between these income sources can help lay down a foundation of financial literacy for children ages six to eight and set them on the path towards becoming millionaires someday.

Understanding Credit Cards, Debit Cards, Checks

If you have a young kid between the ages of six and eight, you may be wondering how to teach them about money. One important way is to explain the differences between credit cards, debit cards, and checks.

Explaining Credit Cards: A credit card is like a loan that lets you borrow money from a bank or other lender. When using a credit card, it is important to pay off the balance each month. Otherwise, interest will be charged on what you owe and your debt can quickly spiral out of control.

Explaining Debit Cards: A debit card links directly to your checking account and allows you to spend money from that account directly. The main benefit of a debit card is that it can help you keep track of your spending as each purchase is immediately deducted from your account.

Explaining Checks: A check is like an IOU that lets you withdraw money from a bank or other lender, which can be done in person at the bank or using online banking. When writing a check, make sure you have enough money in your account to cover the amount of the check. Otherwise, you could be charged a fee and your credit score may suffer if the check bounces.

Teaching young kids about financial literacy starts

with understanding these three basic concepts. By helping them understand how each works, you can set them on the path to becoming a millionaire.

To read more about teaching kids financial literacy, visit the website of your local bank to find out what resources they offer or speak to an advisor. Understanding money and how it works can help children gain independence and security in their lives.

Develop Financial Discipline

Financial discipline is important for kids of all ages, but it's especially important to start instilling these good habits in kids aged six to eight. Developing financial discipline at this age can help set the foundations for a future of financial responsibility and success.

One way to get your children started on developing their financial discipline is to teach them the basics of budgeting. Show your children how to make a budget and explain why it's important to stay within their means. Have regular conversations with them about money and help them understand that it is possible to save up for something they want, but it isn't always possible to buy everything right away.

Another way to help develop financial discipline in kids aged six to eight is to encourage them to give to charity. It's never too early to start teaching children about the importance of giving back and helping those less fortunate than themselves. Consider setting aside a portion of their allowance or other money that they earn for charitable donations, or let them choose a cause they'd like to donate to.

Finally, it's important to teach kids at this age about the power of compounding interest. Explain what interest is and how it can help money grow over time. Have your child set aside money for long-term savings goals and explore ways that they can make their money work hard for them - such as investing in stocks, bonds, and mutual funds.

What Is The Meaning Of The Concept Of Supply And Demand?

The concept of supply and demand is an economic model that explains how prices for goods and services are determined in a free market economy. It states that, when there is a high demand for a product or service, the price will go up; when there is little or no demand, the price will go down. If there is more of a product or service available than what people are willing to pay for it, the price will go down. Likewise, if the product or service is scarce and more people want it than can be supplied, then the price will increase. In essence, supply and demand explain how prices respond to changes in both the quantity of goods and services offered and the number of people willing to purchase them. By understanding this concept, kids can learn how to better manage their money and understand the importance of creating a budget for their expenses. They can also learn the basics of economics by exploring how different factors –

such as availability, demand, and even government policies – influence prices.

Availability

Availability is a key concept for children of all ages to understand when it comes to achieving financial success. Children as young as six can begin understanding how the availability of something, like one's own time and energy, impacts their earning potential. Encourage your kids to think about how their ability to supply goods or services affects what they earn. For example, look for ways to teach them the concept of supply and demand by explaining that if they are able to offer a service or product at a high level and in great demand, their ability to earn more money is greater. This could include taking on extra chores around the house or yard such as mowing the lawn, washing cars, or pet-sitting for the neighbours. Kids can also explore more creative ways to turn their talents and interests into cash, such as setting up a small business online or offering services like tutoring or web design. Teaching kids about the concept of availability and how it impacts their earning potential is an important step in helping them become financially savvy millionaires.

Demand

Demand is one of the most important aspects of becoming a millionaire. It's important to teach kids at this age about supply and demand so that they understand how it works. At this age, kids can start to learn about basic economics such as what creates more demand for certain products or services. This will help them to think strategically when it comes to investing in the future.

By understanding what factors can create more demand for a product or service, kids can learn how to buy and sell items in order to make a profit. They should also understand that demand is relative from region to region as well as depending on the current market conditions. It's important to help them grasp these concepts so they can be prepared to make smart decisions when it comes to investing in their future.

Government Policies

Government policies play a significant role in the financial success of children. Young millionaires need to understand how government policies, such as taxation and tariffs, can influence supply and demand. Knowing this information can help them make more informed decisions when it comes to investments or business ventures. Furthermore, understanding the ways that government policies may affect their bank accounts can help kids plan for their future and make sure that they are always making smart financial decisions.

Another important thing to remember when it comes to government policies is that laws can change at any time. As a result, young millionaires need to stay informed about any changes in the law and how those changes might impact them financially. This way, they can always stay ahead of the game and make sure that their finances are in order. Finally, it's important to note that most government policies will have some sort of an effect on the market and on individual businesses and investors, so understanding them can help kids be better prepared to handle whatever changes come their way.

Overall, mastering the concept of supply and demand and understanding government policies are two key elements to becoming a successful young millionaire. Doing so will help them make sound financial decisions and plan for their future. By educating themselves on these matters, kids can be well on their way to achieving financial success.

Pet Sitting

Pet Sitting is a great small business idea for kids ages six to eight. It can be a fun way for young entrepreneurs to make some extra money while learning responsibility and customer service skills. Plus, they get to spend time with furry friends!

To get started, your little businessperson should create promotional materials like flyers and cards that advertise their services. They should include information such as pricing, what services they offer (like dog walking and feeding), and how to contact them.

Next, the young entrepreneur should figure out how

to market their business. They can hang up flyers in their neighbourhood, spread the word among family and friends, or even set up a website.

Then, it's time for the fun part! Pet Sitting requires a bit of planning and organization. The young entrepreneur should decide which services they are willing to offer, determine the length of visit or walk, create a schedule for pet care visits, and make sure their client's pets receive the best possible care.

Finally, remember that customer service is key. Kids ages six to eight have an opportunity to learn the importance of customer service and how to maintain positive relationships with their clients. They should check in regularly, make sure updates on their progress are communicated, and always provide a safe and enjoyable experience for all involved.

Jewellery Making

Jewellery Making can be a great small business idea for kids between the ages of six and eight. It allows them to express their creativity in fun and colourful ways, while also learning more about crafting and design. With the right materials and tools, they can create custom pieces that will help them generate some extra pocket money or even start up their own small business.

Jewellery Making is an easy craft that can be done with materials like beads, string, wire, and other colourful embellishments. Depending on the age of the child and their experience level, they could make necklaces, bracelets, earrings, or even brooches. For younger children just starting out, it's a great way to learn basic hand-eye coordination and fine motor skills. They can also learn the basics of design, like colour theory, patterns, and shapes.

With a little guidance, children can create something that is unique and maybe even marketable! They could set up a table at local fairs or even have their own online shop to sell their creations to family and friends. This business could help them learn about marketing, inventory tracking, and setting up a pricing system.

Jewellery Making can be an exciting small business idea for kids between the ages of six and eight. With the right materials and tools, they can express their creativity while also learning more about crafting and design. It's a great way to teach them basic hand-eye coordination, fine motor skills, and even the basics of design. Plus, with a little guidance and hard work, they could have their own small business that helps them learn about marketing, inventory tracking, and setting up a pricing system. Don't forget to help them pick out the right materials to get their creative juices flowing!

Selling Homemade Treats

Selling Homemade Treats is a great small business idea for kids ages six to eight. With their parents' help, these young entrepreneurs can create and sell delicious treats like cookies, cakes, cupcakes, and other baked goods.

One way to make money with this business is to take orders from friends and family and then bake the treats in your home kitchen. You can also set up a booth at a community market or festival. This gives kids the opportunity to interact with potential customers and talk about their products.

When running this type of business, it's important for kids to understand basic safety principles like proper handwashing and food handling, as well as safe storage and delivery of their products. It's also important to have parental supervision to make sure everything is done properly.

Kids can also learn to be responsible when it comes to managing their business finances. They should get a head start by creating an accounting system to keep track of costs and income. This will help them understand the importance of budgeting and developing a pricing strategy that allows them to charge enough for their products in order to turn a profit.

Toy Cleaning Service

Toy Cleaning Service is a great business for kids ages six to eight. Starting such a service requires little more than basic cleaning supplies and the motivation to work hard. Kids can start by offering their services in their own neighborhood, or even expanding their reach by advertising online or through word of mouth. After securing customers, they will need to go over the expectations and pricing with them. They should also be sure to stay organized and keep track of their orders.

When cleaning toys, kids should make sure they follow safety procedures. This involves wearing gloves when handling toys that may have been exposed to dirt, dust, or any other hazardous substances. They will also need to inspect the toys for damage before attempting to clean them. After cleaning, kids can dry off the toys with a cloth and properly wrap them up before returning them to the customer.

By offering a Toy Cleaning Service, kids can acquire valuable business skills while also making some pocket money! They'll learn how to market their services and how to interact with customers professionally. Plus, they will be able to see the satisfaction of their work when customers are happy with the results of their service. Not bad for a business that only requires a few basic cleaning supplies and some hard work!

Art & Crafts Sales

Art & Crafts Sales is a great small business idea for kids aged six to eight. This type of venture can be easily set up and managed by the child, with minimal parental guidance or assistance. Most children in this age group have some level of artistic ability, making them ideal candidates for running their own businesses selling art and crafts.

There are many ways a child could go about starting an Arts & Crafts Sales business. Some creative ideas would include setting up a booth at local farmers markets or craft fairs to showcase and sell their artwork, selling through online marketplaces such as Etsy, or even hosting an in-person art show featuring their creations.

These types of businesses are also relatively inexpensive to start and maintain, so they can be quite profitable for the child. Depending on the type of items they are selling, they can likely find supplies at their local craft store or even thrift stores. Not only will this help the child to learn new skills and develop a sense of responsibility, but it might also become a source of steady income for them.

Encouraging your young entrepreneur in an Art & Crafts Sales business can be a great way to teach them important life lessons, such as budgeting, accounting, and marketing. With the right guidance and support from their parents, kids aged six to eight can start on the path of becoming successful small business owners.

CHAPTER 3: KID MILLIONAIRES
AGE 9 TO 11

Ages 9 to 11 is a crucial age for laying the foundation of financial literacy and teaching kids how to become millionaires. There are several strategies parents can use to help their children develop responsible habits and cultivate an entrepreneurial spirit at this young age. One way to start is by introducing children to budgeting basics. Show them how money comes in (income) and goes out (expenses) and explain how to track spending. Explain the importance of saving and investing by setting a clear example through family budgeting habits.

Another way to teach your kids wealth-building skills is to encourage them to start their own businesses or side hustle. For instance, they could set up a lemonade stand, sell homemade crafts, mow lawns, or design websites. This will help them learn how to manage money responsibly while having fun and making a profit.

Finally, you can also introduce children to the stock market. Show them how stocks are bought and sold and explain the concept of risk versus reward with age-appropriate language. Having an understanding of the stock market will serve as an important foundation for future investments.

Prioritize Saving For Yourself

Kids should start to learn how to save money from a young age. This will help them to become more financially responsible later in life because the habit of saving will become ingrained in them. It can be as simple as setting aside a certain portion of their allowance or gifts they receive for saving. Encourage kids at this age to create a piggy bank or other saving jar and make regular deposits. They can also develop a savings plan that has short-term goals (like buying something special with their saved money) and long-term goals (such as contributing to college expenses). Teaching kids the importance of saving will be beneficial in the long run.

Establish A Checking Account And Debit Card For Your Child

Teaching your child the importance of money management is essential to helping them become a millionaire. Setting up a checking account and debit card for your child can be a great way to help them start learning how to manage their own finances. Setting up an account with your local bank or credit union will not only give them access to their own funds, but it will also teach them the basics of budgeting and money management. Having a debit card linked to their account can help your child learn how to responsibly make purchases and allow them to track their spending habits. You can even set up an automatic transfer each month from your own account that will deposit an allowance into your child's checking account — this is a great way to help them understand the concept of saving and investing. As they get older, you can talk with them about setting up a budget and how it can be used as an effective tool to save money. By establishing a checking account and debit card for your child, they will have access to manage their own funds in a responsible manner that will help them become a millionaire.

Future Projections

As your kids move into their teenage years, they will need to start thinking about the future and what career path they would like to take. Encourage them to research different fields that interest them or create a plan for how they can use their skills and interests to pursue their dream job. Show them how to make projections of where they want to be in 5, 10 or 15 years and how they can plan out each step to get there. As they get older, you can also help them understand more about investments and the stock market. You can start small, like having your kids track different stocks and discuss the results with them. This will help provide a basic understanding of investment principles as well as the importance of planning and budgeting.

Once they reach adulthood, you can encourage them to continue learning and investing in different stocks and other financial vehicles. With a little bit of advice from you, they will have all the tools necessary to become successful financially. Additionally, you can introduce them to different business opportunities and help them understand the power of leveraging their time and money for greater returns.

Investment Principles

Investment principles can be taught to children as early as 9 or 10 years old, so they can start understanding the basics of money management and the importance of saving. Kids need to understand that by properly investing their funds, they are setting themselves up for a bright financial future.

When teaching investment principles, it is essential to provide clear examples and easy-to-understand explanations. By teaching kids the basics of stocks, bonds, mutual funds, and other investment vehicles, they can start to build a strong financial foundation. Additionally, it is important to discuss future projections when investing so that kids understand the possible risks associated with certain investments.

Money management skills are essential for young people if they are to become millionaires in the future. Investing is an important part of becoming a millionaire, so teaching kids these principles early on can help them make sound decisions and set themselves up for success. By understanding the basics, they can begin to build their wealth through smart investment strategies.

Understanding The Balance Sheet

Understanding the Balance Sheet is an important step to becoming a millionaire as a kid. To begin, it's important to understand the different components of this financial document. A balance sheet includes assets, liabilities and equity. Assets represent items of value that your child owns such as cash, investments and property. Liabilities are debts or other obligations owed by the business or individual. Equity is the difference between the asset and liability values.

By understanding what assets, liabilities and equity represent, your child can begin to understand how their financial situation works. This includes being able to create a budget, track expenses, save money and invest in the stock market. By doing so, it will help them develop an understanding of how to build and grow wealth.

Another important component of understanding the balance sheet is knowing how to read one. Balance sheets use a simple format that includes listing assets, liabilities and equity on three separate lines. The values for each item are added together at the bottom of the page to give an overall statement of financial position. Kids should have a basic understanding of the accounting equation, which states that assets equal liabilities plus equity.

Finally, understanding the balance sheet is essential for being a successful millionaire kid because it will help them keep track of their personal finances. By knowing what they own and owe, they can create an effective budget and stay on top of their finances. This knowledge is important in order to reach their goal of becoming a millionaire.

Real-Life Living Expenses

Real-life living expenses refer to the expenses that we have in our day-to-day lives. This includes things such as groceries, transportation costs, rent or mortgage payments, utilities, entertainment and more. It can also include investments and other financial tools like savings accounts or stocks. Teaching children about these real-life living expenses will help them understand how to budget their money and what kind of items they should or should not be spending their money on. Knowing the importance of real-life living expenses can help children become millionaires by teaching them how to manage and save their money wisely. Children need to know that in order to achieve financial freedom, they need to consider all aspects of their financial life, from budgeting to investing. And understanding real-life living expenses can help them do just that. By learning the importance of real-life living expenses, children can learn how to set goals and work towards achieving those goals while also staying within a budget. They will be able to use this knowledge to become financially successful in the future and become millionaires. Teaching children how to manage real-life living expenses can be beneficial not only for their financial success but also for their personal development as they learn responsibility, discipline, and a sense of accomplishment.

Credit Scores And Their Importance

Teaching children the importance of credit scores is essential for preparing them to be financially independent adults. A credit score is a numerical value that lenders use to assess a person's likelihood of making payments on time and in full. Several factors go into calculating this score, such as payment history, the total debt owed, length of credit history, types of credit used, and new credit accounts. A good credit score can help kids qualify for loans with lower interest rates, or even no interest at all.

Credit scores begin to form at an early age, so it's important to teach children the fundamentals of using credit responsibly from a young age. Encourage kids to pay off their debts on time each month and not max out their credit cards. Remind them to always read the fine print when signing up for a new credit card or loan and make sure they understand the terms of repayment. Explain how making more than one late payment can cause serious damage to their credit score, and that this could affect future loan applications.

Finally, help kids monitor their credit scores

regularly as it is an essential part of building a secure financial future. While it's unlikely for kids under 18 to have access to their full credit reports, there are other ways that they can check their scores. Encourage them to sign up for free online services that provide basic credit score information or discuss with them the advantages of signing up for a paid subscription service if they want more in-depth data.

Calculating Score

Calculating your credit score is not as difficult as it may seem. It involves looking at the factors that influence your creditworthiness, such as payment history, amount of debt, length of credit history and types of credit used. Payment history is the most important factor in calculating a person's credit score. This means making regular payments on time and in full. The amount of debt you have compared to the total available credit is also important. A low ratio of debt to available credit, such as 30% or less, is generally favoured. The length of your credit history is another factor that impacts your score and more established histories are usually rewarded with higher scores. Lastly, different types of accounts can influence your overall score. Having a mix of credit cards, auto loans and mortgages could be beneficial. It's important to remember that paying off debt is not the same as borrowing responsibly. Paying down balances on existing accounts will not improve your score, but having a history of responsible borrowing will. Taking these steps can help you to build a good credit score which could put you in line for bigger opportunities as an adult.

Payment History

Payment history is an important factor when it comes to building good credit scores. It shows potential lenders how reliable and responsible you are in paying your bills on time. A good payment record can help you get better interest rates when applying for loans or a new line of credit. As children reach their pre-teen years, they should begin to understand the importance of keeping up with payments. Teaching children to set up automatic payments or reminders for bills can help them stay on top of their financial commitments. Additionally, setting up a budget and tracking expenses is also an important way to ensure that the money is there when it's due. Finally, having a savings account with money put aside for emergency expenses is an important factor in maintaining good credit scores. These are all great habits to teach kids as they approach their teenage years.

The Total Debt Owed

The total debt owed is essential to take into consideration when considering how to become a millionaire child. Credit scores are a major factor in debt and can be used to help children understand the importance of being fiscally responsible. Teaching kids about credit scores, how they work, and why maintaining them is important will go a long way toward helping them reach their goal of becoming millionaires. Education on budgeting, cutting debt, and saving regularly is also important topics to discuss when it comes to debt. Having a good understanding of their total debt owed can help children make better decisions regarding money management and future investments. When teaching your child about debt, keep in mind that just because they have a credit score does not mean they need to take on more debt than necessary or accumulate unnecessary interest. Teaching them about managing debt responsibly is key to becoming a millionaire.

Length Of Credit History

A key factor in determining your credit score is your length of credit history. The longer you have a positive, responsible credit history, the higher your score will be. For kids ages 9 to 11, it's unlikely that they will yet have established any type of credit history; however, there are ways to begin building a good foundation even at this young age. One way is to encourage kids to open up a savings account and begin making regular deposits. This will help them become familiar with the concept of banking and start a history of managing their money responsibly, without accruing debt. Additionally, there are age-appropriate financial literacy programs available that could provide valuable lessons about responsible credit management. Teaching children the importance of managing their money and understanding credit at a young age will set them up for success later in life. Encouraging kids to develop good financial habits while they are still young can go a long way towards helping them achieve their goals of becoming a millionaire as an adult.

Types Of Credit Used

Types of credit used can affect a child's credit score. Credit cards, student loans, and other types of debt are all forms of credit that may help to build or damage a child's credit profile. Teaching children about the importance of managing their credit wisely and understanding how different types of credit work are important for their future financial success.

Educating kids about the importance of good credit is essential for them to understand how it relates to their future. Kids should be taught the different types of credit: revolving, instalment, open and closed-end accounts. They should also be made aware of the effects that late payments or missed payments have on their credit score. Teaching children how to use credit responsibly will help them achieve financial success in the future.

Securing An Authorized User Credit Card For Your Child

Having a good credit score is essential for financial success, and it's never too early to start building a positive credit history. If your child is at least nine years old, you may want to consider applying for an authorized user credit card on their behalf.

An authorized user credit card will allow your child to begin building a solid credit score from a young age without having to assume the financial responsibility of a traditional credit card. As an authorized user, your child can make purchases and have their name associated with the account; however, only the main cardholder is held legally responsible for any debt accrued on the account.

You must monitor your child's spending habits carefully when they become an authorized user. Make sure they understand the importance of not going over their spending limit and paying off any credit card bills immediately, as delayed or missed payments can seriously affect their credit score.

Nature Of Borrowing

At ages 9 to 11, children may not necessarily understand the concept of borrowing money. Borrowing money is a financial strategy used when one needs funds and must obtain it from another source in order to cover expenses or make investments. Kids need to learn about what happens when you borrow money, such as interest rates and repayment terms — how much and how often payments are made. Kids should also be taught about the consequences of not making loan repayments, such as late fees and potential credit score damage. This understanding will help equip kids with financial literacy skills to better understand borrowing money later in life.

Another important concept related to borrowing is credit scores, which measure a person's ability to borrow money based on their demonstrated ability to pay it back. Credit scores are based on a person's past credit history and their current financial situation and can range from 300 to 850. Having a good credit score is important when it comes to borrowing money, as higher scores will usually result in lower interest rates, while lower scores can make it more difficult or expensive to borrow money. Kids should learn about the importance of good credit and how to maintain it. Teaching kids about the nature of borrowing and credit scores will set them up for success in their future money management endeavours.

Kids between the ages of 9 and 11 should learn about the importance of having a good credit score and maintaining it as well as the implications of not paying back loans on time. We should also teach them the basics of borrowing money, such as interest rates and repayment terms. By doing so, we can help ensure that they are equipped with the financial literacy skills to handle their finances responsibly in the future.

Gradually Letting Go Of Your Child's Stock Investment Control

When it comes to investing in stocks, the key for kids aged 9 to 11 is gradual steps. Start by giving them the responsibility of researching stocks and understanding how they work. Let your child pick a few stocks and track their performance over time. As they get more comfortable with stock investment, you can give them more control over their investments.

In addition to allowing your child to make decisions, you should also provide guidance. Help them understand the risks associated with stock investment, and encourage them to diversify their portfolio. Show your children how to read stock market performance reports, and teach them about different types of stocks such as growth stocks or value stocks.

Finally, it's important to let go gradually and foster a healthy attitude towards risk-taking. Don't give them access to large sums of money or make them feel like they have to make big returns. Instead, encourage them to take small risks and use their stock investments as a learning experience.

Conducting Thorough Research

Conducting Thorough Research is a key factor in achieving success as a millionaire kid. The research should include looking into different money-making opportunities that are age-appropriate and feasible for the child, such as starting their own business or getting involved in investments. Research should also involve learning about how to manage finances properly and responsibly, including budgeting, saving, and investing wisely. Taking the time to conduct research can help to ensure that the child does not get in over their head or make a costly mistake. Additionally, researching options for earning money can also help to inspire and motivate the child, as they discover new ways to potentially build their fortune.

While conducting research is important, it's also important for kids to have a mentor or advisor who can provide guidance and advice. This could be a family member, teacher, or experienced investor who can offer valuable insights that will help the child make informed decisions for their financial future. Kids should also look to achieve a balance between conducting research and taking risks in order to grow their wealth quickly and responsibly. With proper research and assistance from a mentor/advisor, millionaire kids are sure to be on their way to success.

Party Planning Business

Party Planning Business is a great business idea for kids ages 9 to 11 who want to become millionaires. It involves creativity and problem-solving skills that can help children develop an entrepreneurial mindset. With this type of business, kids get a chance to work on their organizational and communication skills, as well as gain experience in budgeting and marketing. Kids will also learn how to negotiate contracts with clients and set prices for their services. They will also learn the importance of customer service, as well as how to be patient and understanding when dealing with difficult clients. A successful party planning business can help kids develop important life skills that they can carry beyond their childhood years.

When starting a party planning business, it is important to begin by researching what types of events are popular in the local area. After deciding on a type of event, it is then necessary to determine how many hours will be needed to plan and execute the event. Time should also be allocated for preparing marketing materials, such as flyers or brochures, and contacting potential clients. Once customers are secured for an event, the next step is creating a budget that includes all expenses associated with the planning and executing of the event. Finally, kids should also consider hiring staff to help execute the event, such as servers or DJs, if needed.

What Types Of Events Are Popular In The Local Area?

Planning the perfect party can be a daunting task, especially for kids ages 9 to 11. However, with the right knowledge and resources, it is possible to create a fun and entertaining event that everyone will enjoy.

When running a party planning business, it's important to keep up with what types of events are popular in the local area. Depending on the location, different activities and decorations may be more or less desirable for kids of this age. For example, a birthday party in a city might include an outdoor scavenger hunt while one on the beach should focus on water-based activities like swimming or sandcastle building. Popular themes for these events also vary greatly depending on location; they can range from space adventures to animal safaris.

Dog Walking Business

Dog Walking Business can be a great business opportunity for millionaire kids between the ages of 9 to 11. This type of business allows young entrepreneurs to make an income while doing something they love - spending time with animals and being outside. Dog walking businesses typically involve taking a dog or several dogs on walks around the neighbourhood, parks, or other areas of the city. The business involves setting up regular customer services, such as daily or weekly walks. It may also include providing pet sitting services, dog grooming, and other related tasks. Dog-walking businesses can be a great way for young entrepreneurs to build their business skills and gain experience in the industry. Additionally, it can provide them with an opportunity to interact with animal owners and learn how to handle animals responsibly. Running a successful dog-walking business requires dedication, hard work, and attention to detail. It is also important for young entrepreneurs to remain organized and keep track of their finances in order to ensure their business is profitable. With the right skills and resources, millionaire kids between the ages of 9 to 11 can become successful dog-walking business owners.

Painting Faces

Painting Faces is a fun and creative activity that can be enjoyable for both kids and adults. For millionaire kids ages 9 to 11, painting faces can be an exciting activity that allows them to express their creativity and explore their imagination. Painting faces can provide children with a sense of accomplishment as they create something beautiful, while also providing an opportunity to learn about colors and shapes. Kids can use face paints, markers, or even crayons to create unique designs and brighten up their faces. Painting Faces can also be a great way for kids to bond with friends and family as they show off their creative masterpieces.

Parents should ensure that any materials used are non-toxic and age-appropriate, such as washable face paints or hypoallergenic markers, to keep kids safe and healthy. They should also supervise the activity to make sure that kids do not get too carried away with their painting. Painting Faces can provide hours of entertainment and help kids develop artistic skills while having fun!

In addition to being a fun activity for millionaire kids ages 9 to 11, Painting Faces is also a great way to teach children about facial expressions. Kids can explore how to create different emotions on their faces, such as surprise, happiness, and sadness. This helps them understand how people communicate without words and encourages empathy towards others.

Musical Performer

Musical Performer provides a great opportunity for millionaire kids ages 9 to 11 to express their creativity through music. They can learn about composing, singing, and playing instruments. Professional teachers can help young performers develop the skills necessary for success in the music industry. Not only is musical performance excellent for personal growth, but it also helps these millionaires build connections with other people in the industry and hone their business acumen. Musical performance can also help kids develop a sense of confidence and self-worth as they hone their craft over time. It's the perfect way for millionaire kids ages 9 to 11 to explore their creative side while learning about music business fundamentals at the same time.

The parents of millionaire kids should consider enrolling them in music classes or private tutoring. Doing so will help them gain a better understanding of the music industry and hone their performance skills. They can also build relationships with other performers in the industry, which can help open up opportunities for collaborations and performances. Depending on their goals, parents may even want to consider sending their kids to summer camps or master classes that are specifically designed to teach musical performance.

Design T-Shirts

Design T-Shirts are an exciting and creative way for millionaire kids ages 9 to 11 to express themselves. With the help of professional designers, these young entrepreneurs can create unique one-of-a-kind shirts that will make them stand out from the crowd. Design T-Shirts allow kids to explore their creativity and show off their flair for fashion. Not only will they have fun creating something special, but they'll gain valuable experience in the process. With Design T-Shirts, kids will learn how to create a design from start to finish, including selecting fabrics, colours, and patterns and then turning that idea into an actual product. By giving kids a chance to explore their creativity while learning important business skills like marketing and promotion, Design T-Shirts is the perfect way for millionaire kids ages 9 to 11 to get the most out of their entrepreneurial spirit.

With Design T-Shirts, kids can have fun creating something unique and special that will show off their style. Whether they're looking to make a statement or just add a little flair to an outfit, there are so many possibilities with Design T-Shirts. Kids can choose from a variety of colours, fabrics, and styles to create a unique shirt that reflects their personality. From bold graphics to subtle designs, the possibilities are endless! Plus, they'll gain valuable experience along the way by learning how to market and promote their creations.

Lawn-Mowing Service

Millionaire kids aged 9 to 11 can start a lawn-mowing service and make money while having fun! It's a simple business that requires no special skills or tools. All you need is a mower, some fuel and elbow grease. Kids can offer their services to neighbours, family, friends and other local businesses to get their businesses up and running quickly. They can charge by the hour or as a flat fee per job and use their earnings to buy more mowing equipment, fuel, or even save for college! This is a great way to teach kids about business and money management while having fun outside. Plus, they'll be doing something useful in their community. So why not give it a try? Who knows – you could have the next millionaire kid on your hands!

Mastering The Income Statement

Mastering the Income Statement is one of the key elements to becoming a millionaire at any age. For kids ages 9 to 11, this can be accomplished by teaching them the basics of financial literacy —such as budgeting and saving money—as early as possible. Encouraging children to open their own bank accounts and record expenses on a regular basis can help instil an understanding of how money works and the importance of being financially responsible. Additionally, introducing the concept of investing in stocks or other long-term investments at an early age can help kids begin to understand the power of compounding returns and how even small amounts saved can add up over time.

Finally, teaching kids about businesses—including how they work and how to start one—can help them build the skills necessary to start their own businesses. By exposing children to the fundamentals of business ownership, they can begin learning about entrepreneurship and what it takes to succeed in today's competitive marketplace. Ultimately, by teaching kids the basics of financial literacy, investing, and entrepreneurship early on, they'll be more likely to become millionaires later in life.

With the right guidance, kids age 9 to 11 can start developing money-management skills that will serve them well into adulthood. With a strong foundation in the basics of financial literacy and an understanding of how businesses work, they'll have the knowledge and confidence needed to build wealth over time. For parents, this means starting the conversation and setting an example of smart money management from a young age. With patience and dedication, kids can become millionaires and live comfortable lives as adults.

Home Organization Services

Kids aged 9 to 11 could help their local community by providing organizational services that are tailored to meet every family's needs. This could involve anything from organizing bedrooms, closets, playrooms and other living spaces in a way that maximizes efficiency and creates space. By offering these services, kids can help their local community stay organized and make more efficient use of space. Furthermore, the skills learned through this kind of business could be honed and used in other areas of life such as school or college coursework. It's a great way for young entrepreneurs to get experience in the business world while at the same time helping those around them.

By setting up a website or social media page, kids can easily advertise their services and start to build a client base. They can also reach out to local families in person and let them know about the kind of services they offer. This could potentially turn into an incredibly successful venture for any young entrepreneur.

Through this kind of business, kids will learn how to be organized, develop problem-solving skills, and gain valuable experience with customer service. All of these are important traits for any successful businessperson to have, and kids can start honing their own skills early. This is a great way to make some pocket money while learning life lessons that will be invaluable in the long run.

Organizing services can be incredibly helpful for

families, so it's no surprise that these kinds of businesses can be successful. If you have an entrepreneurial kid between the ages of 9 to 11, this is a great way for them to get started on their business journey and start making money!

Grocery Shopping

Small Business Ideas for Kids is an excellent small business idea for kids aged 9 to 11. It can be a great way for them to learn about budgeting, nutrition, and customer service. They can start by offering weekly grocery shopping services to neighbours or family members. They can work out a price list in advance that covers the cost of groceries plus delivery fees. They may even have the opportunity to familiarize themselves with some of the products on the shelves and become more comfortable with food labels. This activity also provides them with an opportunity to practice their math skills by calculating prices, making changes, and keeping records of transactions. Overall, grocery shopping can be a great way for kids aged 9 to 11 to develop both business acumen and practical life skills.

Car Detailing

Car detailing is the process of thoroughly cleaning, restoring and finishing a car's interior and exterior components. The goal of detailing is to make the car look as close to new as possible, while preserving its longevity. Detailing involves everything from washing and waxing to polishing and protecting all parts of the vehicle. It also includes vacuuming, steam cleaning, and applying protective products such as sealants and waxes. Car detailing can be done both on the interior and exterior of the car to give it a refreshed look. For kids ages 9-11, car detailing could make an excellent small business idea as they learn more about cars and become better at their craft. As kid entrepreneurs in the world of car detailing, they can develop their own car cleaning products, and offer services such as waxing, window tinting, and paint corrections for cars in their neighbourhood. It is important to note that kids should always work with adult supervision when attempting any car detailing services. Additionally, it is crucial to check the laws of your state or country before starting a business like this. With the right guidance and training, car detailing could be a lucrative business venture for kids ages 9-11.

Housecleaning

Housecleaning can be a great business venture for kids aged 9 to 11. It's an easy way to earn money, and it teaches children valuable skills like responsibility, organization, and hard work. Setting up the business is relatively straightforward: create flyers advertising your services, set prices based on the type of cleaning required (e.g., vacuuming or laundry), and offer a variety of other services such as window washing or carpet cleaning. Don't forget to include liability insurance in case of accidents. When it comes to house cleaning, safety is key: make sure kids are equipped with the right tools and know which products to use for different surfaces. Encourage them to wear gloves and masks when necessary. You can even have the kids team up for larger jobs to increase their earning potential.

Plant Care

Plant Care can be a great small business opportunity for kids ages 9 to 11. Plant care involves caring for plants, including watering, pruning, fertilizing, and repotting them. It also involves diagnosing plant diseases and identifying pests that may be damaging plants. Kids who are interested in this business should start by learning the basics of plant care and selecting a speciality like flowering or houseplants.

Once the basics and speciality are mastered, kids can begin marketing their services. They may want to start by offering their services to family and friends, then branch out into the wider community. Kids should also consider joining local gardening clubs or other related organizations to learn more about plant care and expand their network of customers.

In addition to providing basic services, kids could offer their customers consulting advice on how to take better care of their plants. They could also offer classes or workshops in plant care to further expand their business.

By taking the right steps and providing quality

service, kids can turn plant care into a successful small business venture. It's an excellent opportunity for them to learn not only about the plants themselves, but also about running a business and customer service.

Errands Runner

Errands Runner is an ideal small business for kids aged 9 to 11. It involves running simple errands, such as grocery shopping and delivering items locally. This type of business offers a great way to become more independent and learn important skills like customer service, communication, responsibility, money management and more.

When starting an errands and running the business, it's important to keep safety in mind. Make sure your child is comfortable running errands alone and that he/she understands basic safety precautions like staying in well-lit, populated areas and using proper pedestrian signals. It's also a good idea to limit the amount of money your child carries when out running errands.

To get started, kids need to build a customer base. Reach out to family members and neighbours to see if they need any errands run. Offer a discount for new customers to encourage word-of-mouth advertising. To keep track of tasks, it may be helpful to set up a simple spreadsheet with deadlines and expectations.

Kids should also consider charging an appropriate rate for their services. It's important to remember that young entrepreneurs are dealing with people who are likely paying for convenience. Setting the rates too low may lead customers to believe that the services offered lack value.

Errands running is a great opportunity for kids aged 9 to 11 to take on responsibility, learn valuable business skills, and even make some money while having fun. Be sure to set expectations, establish safety protocols, manage finances appropriately and keep track of tasks, and you'll be on your way to running a successful errands business.

Handyman Services

Handyman Services is a great small business opportunity for kids between the ages of 9 and 11. These services can include basic home repairs, such as painting, replacing lightbulbs, repairing small appliances, or fixing furniture. Depending on their skill level and comfort level with tools, they may also be able to perform more complex tasks like changing door locks or assembling furniture from kits.

These services can be offered to neighbours or family members, allowing kids to gain valuable experience while earning some extra money. Kids should also know their limits when it comes to offering these services and should never attempt a job they are not qualified for. They must stay safe and use proper safety equipment at all times.

In addition to traditional handyman services, kids can also offer lawn care services or snow shovelling.

These jobs are great for earning money in a short amount of time and require minimal tools or supplies. Kids can also look into offering pet-sitting services as another way to make some extra cash.

CHAPTER 4: KID MILLIONAIRES
AGE 12 TO 15

Ages 12 to 15 are the perfect time to start teaching kids about money and building wealth. There are a variety of ways that parents, guardians, and mentors can help children in this age range develop smart financial habits so they can become millionaires before they turn 18.

One great way to get started is by discussing the power of compound interest with your child. Compound interest is a powerful force that can help turn small investments into larger amounts of money over time. Kids need to understand how compound interest works and the importance of starting early when it comes to investing.

Another way to help kids become millionaires is by teaching them about the stock market and investing. At ages 12 to 15, kids don't need to invest in real stocks as there are plenty of online simulations that allow them to get an idea of how the stock market works. Showing them how to research stocks, read financial statements, and make educated decisions when it comes to investing can help prepare them for success in their future investments.

Finally, teaching your child about entrepreneurship is a great way to introduce them to the world of wealth-building. Having an understanding of business and finance concepts at a young age can help them identify potential opportunities to monetize their ideas. As they get older, you can even accompany them on visits to local businesses to show how real-world entrepreneurs are making money in a variety of ways.

Businesses

businesses are a great way for millionaire kids aged 12 to 15 to make money. With the help of parents, guardians or mentors, young entrepreneurs can create their own companies in an array of industries and generate income through various activities such as selling products online, offering services like tutoring or babysitting, creating apps, etc.

Besides making money from businesses they created themselves, kids can also get involved in existing businesses either as an investor or partners. They can use the money they've earned to invest in stocks and bonds, real estate, or other business opportunities.

Making money through businesses is a great way for kids to gain financial literacy and build wealth. Having their own source of income allows them to understand the value of hard work and gain valuable experience in the business world.

Finally, having businesses also allows kids to give back by donating a portion of their income to causes they care about and help those in need. Through their businesses, kids can become an example for other young people and teach them how to build wealth responsibly.

Getting involved in businesses from an early age is an excellent way for millionaire kids to make money and gain experience in the business world. Whether it's starting their own companies or investing in existing businesses, these activities can help young entrepreneurs achieve financial success and teach them important skills that will benefit them throughout their lives.

Budget Wisely And Increase Your Income

It is important for children in the age range of 12 to 15 to learn the importance of budgeting and how to increase their income. By budgeting wisely, kids can get a better handle on their money and maximize their earnings. Kids can start by writing down all of their expenses each month, such as bills, food, entertainment, etc. This will help them to better understand how much money they have coming in and how much is going out. Additionally, kids at this age should look for ways to increase their income by taking on part-time jobs or completing online tasks. This could include things such as tutoring other students, walking neighbours' dogs, mowing lawns, and completing freelance tasks.

Tutoring Other Students

Tutoring other students is a great way for kids ages 12-15 to start building their wealth. Tutoring allows them to put the skills they already have to work and earn extra income. Kids in this age range need to budget wisely so that they can save as much of this money as possible. This means setting aside a portion of their earnings each month and investing it in something that will grow over time.

When setting up their tutoring sessions, it's important for kids to create a schedule that works best for them, and to also ask for payment upfront. This way, they don't have to worry about chasing after people who owe them money. Additionally, kids in this age range need to advertise themselves as tutors to ensure that they are reaching the most people possible.

Tutoring is a great way for kids ages 12-15 to start building their wealth while also helping other students learn and grow. With a bit of planning, budgeting, and marketing savvy, these kids can set themselves up for success as they continue on their journey towards becoming millionaires.

Mowing Lawns

Mowing lawns is a great way for millionaire kids aged 12 to 15 to increase their income. With some basic gardening tools, they can easily advertise their services in the neighbourhood and start making money right away. They should also budget wisely so they can save up as much money as possible. When it comes to spending, kids should think about what items or experiences will add value to their lives rather than buying something just because it looks cool. They should also be aware of what their biggest expenses are so they can make sure to prioritize them and allocate enough money for them. By budgeting wisely, kids can ensure that they have enough money left over each month to invest in themselves or put towards their savings. With some hard work and dedication, millionaire kids aged 12 to 15 can learn to be financially responsible and build a bright financial future.

Completing Freelance Tasks

Completing freelance tasks is one of the best ways for kids aged 12 to 15 to increase their income. It requires creativity and problem-solving skills, which can help them develop in other aspects of life as well. When looking for freelance tasks, it's important to research potential employers thoroughly so that you know you're getting paid fairly. Additionally, if a task requires more time and effort than expected, make sure to negotiate for better pay. To complete the tasks successfully, it's important to set realistic expectations for yourself as well as plan out your scheduled time, so that you can get the job done efficiently. With a bit of hard work and perseverance, completing freelance tasks can be a great way to increase your income and save for the future.

Launch A Modern Lemonade Stand

Launching a modern lemonade stand is a great way for kids aged 12 to 15 to start learning how to become a millionaire. By taking the classic concept of running a lemonade stand and adding an entrepreneurial twist, kids can get creative with their ideas and create something that not only earns them money but also teaches them important money-making skills like marketing, financial planning, and customer service.

First, kids should plan out the details of their lemonade stand. They can decide on a catchy name, pick a location (preferably one with lots of foot traffic), and think about what type of lemonade they want to offer (fresh-squeezed or store-bought) and how much they'll charge for each cup. They should also consider possible add-ons like selling snacks or offering free samples to attract customers.

Once the plan is in place, kids can start building the lemonade stand itself. With a few pieces of wood, some paint or contact paper, and an old folding table or piece of plywood, kids can easily create something that looks professional and inviting. For added flair, they can hang a sign or banner with their lemonade stand's logo, motto, or other branding materials.

Offer Babysitting Services

Babysitting is a great way for kids ages 12 to 15 to make extra money and build work experience. It can also be a fun and rewarding job. To become a successful babysitter, you will need to show responsibility and confidence in your abilities. Be sure to brush up on basic first-aid skills too! Start off by advertising your services on local websites or community boards. Additionally, word of mouth is a great tool to spread the news about your babysitting services. Once you start getting calls for jobs, remember to always be punctual and show up with a friendly attitude. Before taking on any job, make sure to discuss the expectations ahead of time so that there are no surprises when it comes time to pay.

Design And Sell Print-On-Demand Products

Design and sell print-on-demand products is a great way for 12 to 15-year-old kids to become millionaires. With the help of online platforms like Society6 and Redbubble, kids can upload their own artwork in any format and turn it into physical products such as t-shirts, mugs, pillows, phone cases, bags etc. These products are then printed on demand when someone purchases them from the child's online store, and the child receives a commission for each sale. This is a great way for kids to start their own businesses and make money without any upfront cost or risk. Plus, it can be done in the comfort of their own home and with minimal supervision from parents or guardians.

With hard work and dedication, these kids could very well become millionaires by selling their print-on-demand products.

By using creative and proven marketing tactics, such as creating attractive social media campaigns and continuously updating their collections, kids can quickly grow their customer base and increase sales. Additionally, kids should make sure to research the pricing of similar products available online in order to create competitive prices for their own designs. By offering high-quality products at competitive prices, kids can ensure that their business will be successful.

Start A Neighbourhood Services Business

Kids of any age can start a business providing services to their neighbours such as lawn mowing, pet walking, snow shovelling, leaf raking or washing cars. They can advertise their business by going door-to-door and giving out flyers in the neighbourhood.

Once they have a few customers they could expand their services by offering other tasks such as gardening, house cleaning, or babysitting. This is a great way for kids to make some extra money and learn the basic principles of running a business. Teaching children about financial responsibility and entrepreneurial skills early on can set them up for success in the future.

Parents should encourage their children to create goals in order to stay motivated and measure their progress. They can also help by giving advice and teaching them about the importance of budgeting, advertising, and customer service. With a little hard work and guidance, kids can become millionaires by the time they reach their teenage years.

Become An Online Creator

This is a great way for kids to become millionaires at a young age. Kids can create videos, podcasts, or blogs with content related to their interests that are likely to get attention from viewers, listeners, or readers. After building an audience base, they can start selling merchandise related to their channel or blog such as t-shirts, hats, mugs, and more. If they are able to build a large enough following, the profits from the sales can add up quickly! By creating content that their audience loves, kids can become millionaires in no time.

Another great tip is to create multiple streams of income by launching their own products or services related to their channel or blog's topics. This could include books, online courses, or exclusive memberships. Kids can also use their content to attract advertisers, sponsors, and other brands who are willing to pay for exposure to their products and services through the channel or blog. All these strategies can help kids become millionaires in a short period of time.

Finally, kids should make sure to take advantage of all the tools and resources available to them online. There are many platforms out there that offer helpful advice and tutorials on how to become an online creator, monetize a channel or blog, and promote their content. Kids should take the time to learn more about these tools and resources so they can make the most of their efforts!

Sell Handmade Goods

Sell handmade goods at a local flea market or online. Encourage your kid to create items such as jewellery, clothing, home decor, and more. Many websites provide easy-to-follow instructions for how to make handmade items. Additionally, these same websites often offer tips on marketing and pricing the products so your kid can maximize their profits. Have them set up a booth at a local flea market or create an online store on websites such as Etsy. This is a great way for kids to learn how to set up their own small business and make some extra money, while also honing creativity.

Also, consider talking to local stores and seeing if they'd be interested in stocking your kid's products. Not only will this give them the experience of working with a store, but it could also be extremely profitable. Additionally, let your kid manage their own finances; have them set aside some money for savings and investments as well as allocate funds for their allowance and future purchases. This will help kids learn how to handle large sums of money responsibly from an early age.

Have your kids think outside the box and look for creative ways to make money. Whether it's starting their own business, doing odd jobs around the neighbourhood, or finding low-cost ways to invest in stocks, there are many opportunities available for young people to become millionaires.

Start A Pet-Care Business

This is an ideal business for kids ages 12 to 15, as they are usually responsible and can handle the responsibility of taking care of animals. Pet-care services can be anything from walking dogs to feeding cats or boarding pets overnight in their home. To set up a pet-care business, first consider the types of services you want to offer and determine a price list for those services. You may also want to talk to a professional, like a vet or pet store owner, to get advice and tips on how to best run your business and provide quality care for your customers' pets. After that, work to market the services you are offering by creating flyers and posting them in the neighbourhood or advertising online. Finally, make sure all of your necessary safety measures are in place, such as being certified in pet first aid and CPR or having the proper permits if needed. With a little bit of determination and hard work, running a pet-care business can be an incredibly rewarding and lucrative opportunity for kids ages 12 to 15.

Host A Pop-Up Market For Youth

It's a great way for young entrepreneurs to learn

how to make money with age-appropriate activities like selling baked goods, crafts, or other products. Offer a percentage of the proceeds from each sale to the child so that they can use their earnings as seed money for future business ventures or other investments. Provide advice and mentorship along the way so that they can learn the basics of running a business. Encourage them to think outside the box and come up with unique ways of selling their products. This can also be an opportunity for kids to get creative and show off their talents or interests in a fun, accessible way. Teach your young entrepreneurs basic money management skills like budgeting and saving so that they can make more informed decisions about how to manage their profits. In addition, let them know the importance of giving back by donating a portion of their profits to charitable causes. Hosting a pop-up market for youth is an empowering way for kids to start building skill sets and a financial portfolio that will help them become millionaires in the future.

Record Reviews And Unboxings For Youtube

Record reviews and unboxings for YouTube are a great way for kids ages 12 to 15 to make money. This is an excellent platform to earn extra cash from the comfort of their own home. By creating videos of products they already own or reviewing products they've tested out, kids can start earning money right away! They can even team up with brands and get paid by them for sponsored reviews and unboxing. This is a great way to learn about different products and gain knowledge while earning some cash at the same time.

These videos can also be monetized through advertising, which is one of the best ways to start making money with YouTube. Kids can set up their own channels and post videos regularly in order to build an audience base and attract more viewers. The key here is to create quality content that people are interested in and will be willing to watch. With consistent effort, kids are sure to start making decent money from YouTube.

Moreover, with the right amount of hard work and dedication, they can even grow their channel and turn it into a full-fledged business. From managing sponsorships, creating merchandize or pushing other products, they can make a lot of money if they are willing to put in the time and effort.

Run A Summer Camp For Younger Kids

Kids aged 12 to 15 can make money quickly by running a summer camp for younger children. This can be done in the neighbourhood, park, or backyard. It can also be done online through video-conferencing and other virtual activities. Charging an hourly fee for each child's participation is a great way to generate income quickly. Activities that could be included in the summer camp include arts and crafts, sports, outdoor games, science experiments, and more.

It is important to ensure that all safety protocols are

followed and that the children attending the camp are supervised by an adult at all times. Setting up a website or social media page where parents can find out more information about your camp is also beneficial. Advertising your services through local publications, flyers and even word-of-mouth will help to spread the word and attract more customers.

Design Websites And Online Stores

If your kid is tech-savvy, he or she can design websites and online stores for businesses in the local area looking to get more customers online. By designing their website, they'll gain valuable experience learning coding languages like HTML, CSS, JavaScript, and PHP as well as e-commerce platforms like Shopify. Doing this type of work can also potentially give your kid a salary of up to $50 per hour! Another great thing about website designing is that they don't need a lot of capital to start, just time and dedication. Furthermore, this activity can build their portfolio, helping them land better jobs in the future.

When it comes to online stores, depending on which e-commerce platform you use, you can easily create a store without having to invest in stock or inventory upfront. Your kid can start their own business and sell items like books, accessories, and other small items that are popular with teenagers. They can spend time marketing the products on social media sites like Instagram or Facebook for free which helps them spread the word about their business and attract more customers. Doing this type of work can also potentially give your kid a salary of up to $50 per hour.

Understanding Taxes

For kid millionaires age 12 to 15, it is important to understand taxes and how they work. Taxes can have a big impact on your finances, so it's important to understand the basics of taxation. To help with this, kids should research and learn about different types of taxes such as income tax, sales tax, property tax, etc. Additionally, understanding how deductions and credits work can help significantly reduce the amount of taxes owed. Knowing how to accurately estimate and file your taxes is also important. Ultimately, understanding taxes can be the difference between having a large tax bill or not! Additionally, learning about financial strategies such as tax-loss harvesting can potentially save hundreds or thousands in taxes each year. To learn more about taxes and other finance topics, kids should look for books, podcasts, and other resources to help them understand the basics. Once they have a good understanding of taxes, it is important to stay informed with current tax laws and regulations as they can change frequently.

Income Tax

Income tax is an important concept to understand for young millionaires. Knowing how to properly pay and file taxes can be complicated and overwhelming, but it's a necessary part of understanding the financial side of business success. A kid millionaire should understand their tax obligations as well as any deductions available to them to ensure they can keep more of their hard-earned money. It's important to consider seeking professional tax advice since the laws are always changing. Additionally, some young millionaires may be eligible for specific deductions based on their age and or income levels. It's also critical for young millionaires to know when their taxes are due and how to file them properly. Understanding taxes can be a complicated process, but with guidance, kids aged 12 to 15 can become knowledgeable about their tax obligations and deductions. Knowing this information will be essential for future business success.

Also, kid millionaires should know that it is illegal to not pay taxes on income earned, and failure to do so could result in serious consequences. Young millionaires need to stay up-to-date with changes in the tax code and consult with a professional tax advisor to ensure they are in compliance. A good understanding of income tax is essential for any successful business, so young millionaires must become knowledgeable about the subject as soon as possible.

Sales Tax

Sales tax is an important concept for kids ages 12

to 15 to understand when it comes to the path towards becoming a millionaire. Sales tax is a type of consumption tax that is added to items that are purchased. It is collected by the seller from the buyer at the time of purchase and remitted to their respective government or other taxing authority. Depending on where you live, sales tax rates may vary from 0% to over 10%. When a purchase is made, the amount of tax charged is determined by the total cost of the item and the applicable rate for that location.

It's important to note that not all goods are subject to sales tax. In some states, certain items such as groceries and medication are not taxable at all. Other states may exempt certain items such as clothing, books, and other essential items from sales tax. Kids age 12 to 15 need to understand which goods are taxable and how much they can expect to pay in taxes on their purchases so that they can plan for it ahead of time.

Understanding sales tax is an important part of becoming a millionaire because it can significantly increase the cost of goods that you purchase. By understanding which items are taxable and how much tax you may be expected to pay, kids age 12 to 15 can make more informed decisions about their purchases and plan accordingly for taxes on their purchases.

Property Taxes

Young entrepreneurs aged 12 to 15 can use property

taxes as a way to become millionaires. Property tax is a type of levy imposed on real estate that must be paid by the owner of the property. It is based on the value of the real estate and can be used to fund local services, such as infrastructure or education. Understanding how to manage property taxes is a crucial part of financial literacy for young entrepreneurs.

When looking at property taxes, it's important to understand the laws and regulations in your area. Each jurisdiction has different rules about how much tax is collected from homeowners or businesses that own real estate. Knowing these rules can help young entrepreneurs make informed decisions about their investments.

It's also important for young entrepreneurs to understand how to use property taxes as an investment tool. Property taxes can be used to increase the value of a property. For example, investing in improvements such as landscaping or adding extra amenities like air conditioning can often result in increased tax deductions from the local government. Additionally, properties with higher land values generally have lower taxes than those with lower values. Understanding these principles can help young entrepreneurs use property taxes as a way to increase their wealth.

Finally, young entrepreneurs need to understand how to minimize the impact of property taxes on their investments. Many jurisdictions offer tax exemptions for certain types of properties, such as those owned by seniors or disabled individuals. Additionally, some jurisdictions allow homeowners to pay taxes on a sliding scale, depending on their income level. Exploring these options can help young entrepreneurs reduce the amount of taxes they have to pay and increase their investment returns.

Estate Taxes

Estate taxes can be complicated but understanding them is important to becoming a millionaire as a kid. Essentially, estate taxes are the taxes that must be paid on assets when someone dies. Depending on the state you live in, there may be varying levels of taxation and exemptions for certain types of assets. It's important to understand how estate taxes work before investing in any high-value assets. Estate taxes can be avoided in some cases, such as through gifting or trusts. It's important to consult a financial advisor or tax professional to understand how estate taxes would apply to your particular situation.

Estate planning is an important part of amassing wealth and kids ages 12 to 15 need to start thinking about how they can minimize their estate tax burden. Understanding taxes and estate taxes is a key step towards becoming a millionaire as a kid.

Distinguishing Assets And Liabilities

Distinguishing Assets and Liabilities is a critical part

of becoming a millionaire at any age, and especially for kids. Assets are anything that could be used to generate income such as businesses, investments, or even properly utilized allowance money. Liabilities are anything that costs money such as debt, expensive toys, or impulse buys. Teaching kids the difference between what is making them money and what is costing them money will help them become more mindful of their spending and investments. Education is key to helping kids differentiate between assets and liabilities, so teaching them basic financial lessons such as budgeting, saving, investing, and debt management should be a priority. Additionally, having discussions about options for generating income such as starting a business or getting involved in stocks can open up opportunities for money-making endeavours that can help them become millionaires. It is important to make sure kids understand the importance of distinguishing assets and liabilities in order to keep their finances on track for future success.

By teaching kids at an early age how to distinguish between assets and liabilities, they will be able to maximize their money-making potential and become millionaires by the time they reach adulthood. With a combination of financial education, discussions about ways to generate income, and self-control when it comes to spending, kids can achieve their dreams of becoming millionaires.

Differentiating Good Debt From Bad Debt

Differentiating Good Debt from Bad Debt is an important concept for kids ages 12 to 15 to understand. Good debt can be used to help build wealth while bad debt can lead to financial difficulty. Kids must understand the difference between the two and how to use debt responsibly.

Good debt, such as taking out student loans or getting a mortgage loan, can provide long-term benefits when managed properly. Good debt helps to build financial security by providing access to education, purchasing a home, or starting a business. With good debt, the amount of interest paid is typically lower than with bad debt and the loan should be used for an asset that will appreciate in value over time.

Bad debt is when money is borrowed for items that don't increase in value and have high-interest rates. Examples of bad debt include credit cards, payday loans, and car title loans. These forms of debt can be dangerous because they are difficult to pay off with the amount of interest that is charged. Kids need to understand that not all debt is created equal and it is best to avoid bad debt as much as possible.

Initiate A Stock Simulator For Your Child's Learning

Stock simulators are a great way to start teaching your child about the stock market. With the help of a stock simulator, kids can build financial literacy and gain an understanding of how to invest in stocks without any real-world risk. To get started, research reputable online brokers that offer kid-friendly trading platforms with educational tools. These may include tutorials and quizzes to help your child understand the basics of stocks, bonds, and mutual funds. Then, open a practice account with "pretend money" for your child to use in simulated stock trades. This way, they can get familiar with how the stock market works without risking any real money. Helping kids learn about investing through the use of a stock simulator will give them invaluable skills they can use later in life.

Additionally, you can provide them with books and videos about the stock market to further enhance their understanding of the fundamentals. This will help them build a solid foundation for long-term financial success.

Investing

Investing is one of the best ways for kids ages 12 to 15 to become millionaires. To get started, kids should familiarize themselves with the stock market and understand how it works. They can start by opening a brokerage account with a bank or online broker and begin researching potential investments. Investing in stocks allows kids to diversify their portfolios and potentially make more money than other types of investments. Additionally, investing in stocks gives kids the opportunity to learn about business and finance at a young age.

Once they have opened their brokerage accounts, kids can start researching and selecting stocks that fit into their portfolios. To make sure they are making smart decisions, they need to read up on financial news and understand the inner workings of the stock market. As kids become more experienced investors, they can also explore other types of investments such as bonds, mutual funds, and ETFs.

Investing can be a great way for kids to make their money work for them and become millionaires. However, they must understand the risks associated with investing and keep their portfolios diversified in order to reduce losses. Additionally, they should always do their own research and consult with a financial advisor before making any investment decisions. With the right knowledge and planning, kids can make smart investments and become millionaires by the time they're 15.

The key to becoming a millionaire as a kid is not only about investing wisely but also about learning how to manage money. Money management skills can help kids develop a budget, save money, and make sure their money is working for them. Additionally, teaching kids the importance of managing their finances will also equip them with the skills they need to be successful adults. Investing in stocks and other investments are great ways for kids to become millionaires, but learning how to manage their money is just as important.

Bonds

Bonds are a great way for kids to get started investing. It's important to understand the different types of bonds available and how they work before investing in them. In general, there are two main categories of bonds: government-backed and corporate-issued. Government-backed bonds often offer lower risk but have lower returns, while corporate-issued bonds may offer higher returns but carry more risk. Kids should start with government-backed bonds since the risk is lower but they can work their way up to more complex investments. To help make bond investing easier, parents can research different types of bonds and set up a custodial account for their children where they can buy and sell bonds. This will teach them how to invest in a practical setting while still offering protection from the risks of investing.

It's important to ensure that your kid understands how interest works and what their bond investments will yield over time. They should also understand the importance of diversifying their investments, so it's a good idea to look into a mix of government and corporate bonds as well as other types of investments such as stocks or mutual funds.

Mutual Funds

Mutual Funds are an excellent way for young people to invest their money. They offer a diversified portfolio of stocks, bonds, and other investments to help your child mitigate risk. The key is to get started early—the longer they have their money invested, the more time it can compound in value and earn potential returns.

A good place to start is with a Roth IRA, which allows your child to contribute after-tax dollars that will then grow tax-free. It also has some essential protection against creditors and bankruptcy. Investing in a mutual fund is relatively simple and can be done online quickly. You'll want to look for funds with low fees and good ratings from independent research organizations like Morningstar or Kiplinger.

Trading Platforms

Trading Platforms can be an excellent way for 12 to 15-year-old millionaire kids to invest their money. Trading platforms allow users to buy, sell, and trade stocks with real-time market data, which allows them to make informed decisions about their investments. These platforms provide tools such as charts, technical analysis, and news feeds that help the user understand pricing trends and identify entry/exit points. Additionally, these platforms offer research capabilities and provide access to a variety of different asset classes, like forex, futures, and options. Furthermore, some platforms even offer educational resources to help users learn more about the markets. By utilizing trading platforms, 12 to 15-year-old millionaire kids can gain the knowledge and experience needed to make wise investment decisions.

Trading Platforms also offer risk management features to help protect users from excessive losses. For example, some platforms provide a variety of order types, such as stop loss orders, limit orders, and trailing stops that enable users to reduce their risk by automatically setting predetermined exit points. Additionally, most platforms offer margin accounts which give users the ability to borrow money to invest more than they have in their accounts.

Exploring The Benefits Of Real Estate Investment

Exploring the Benefits of Real Estate Investment is becoming increasingly popular among young people, including kids as young as millionaires. In this article, we'll discuss why real estate investing can be so beneficial for them and how it can help them build wealth faster than other investments.

Real estate investment offers a variety of benefits that are not available through traditional investments such as stocks and bonds. For example, with real estate, investors have the potential to generate a passive income that can provide long-term financial stability. Additionally, real estate investments can be leveraged to increase profits as well as reduce risk.

Real estate also has the potential for capital growth – meaning that the value of your investment grows over time. This makes it an attractive option for those looking to build wealth over the long term. Real estate investments can also provide tax benefits, such as deductions for mortgage interest and property taxes.

Millionaire kids who invest in real estate can capitalize on these advantages while still having the freedom to pursue their other life goals. By investing in something that will appreciate over time, young millionaires can develop financial stability early on and begin building wealth before they even enter the workforce.

Real estate can provide a great opportunity for kids to begin their journey towards financial success. With the right knowledge and guidance, millionaire kids can use real estate investments to start creating a more secure future for themselves and their families. Investing in real estate is not only an excellent way to build wealth, but it is also a fun and exciting way to explore the world of finance. Investing in real estate can give kids a better understanding of how money works and how they can use it to their advantage.

Encouraging Your Child To Set Up A Car Fund

Encouraging Your Child to Set Up a Car Fund can be a great way to teach them financial responsibility and the importance of goal setting. Start by talking with your child about why they want a car, how much it will cost, and what type of car they would like to own. Then discuss where the money for the car is going to come from - saving, investing, taking out a loan - and provide guidance on how to save and budget for it.

Once your child has determined their goal, make it even more real by helping them open a savings account specifically for the car fund, and show them how they can track their progress towards the goal through online banking tools. Make sure to explain the importance of saving regularly and investing wisely so that they can reach their goal faster. You could also provide tips for budgeting, such as cutting back on unnecessary spending or finding ways to make extra money.

Be sure to reward your child's hard work and dedication by celebrating milestones and acknowledging their achievements along the way. You can do this with small rewards when they hit certain goals or even plan a trip together when they have saved enough money for a car. By doing this, you can help your child realize the importance of setting and reaching goals, while also teaching them important money management skills.

CHAPTER 5 INVESTING FOR THE FUTURE

Encourage entrepreneurship in kids
Entrepreneurship is the process of innovating, creating, and managing a business or organization in order to make a profit. It involves taking risks and finding creative solutions to problems in order to succeed. Teaching kids entrepreneurship can help them develop skills that will benefit them later in life.

Encouraging entrepreneurship in kids is an important step towards helping them become millionaires at a young age. Teaching entrepreneurship to kids can help them understand the basics of how businesses work and help foster creative thinking in them. It can also teach them about the importance of taking risks and being persistent in achieving their goals, both of which are important qualities for any entrepreneur.

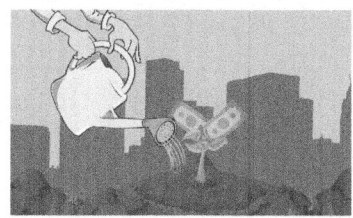

Encourage entrepreneurship in kids by introducing them to concepts such as business management, networking, money management, marketing and planning. Help kids develop an understanding of the basics of operating a business with real-life examples and teach them how to identify potential profit opportunities. Allow kids to make mistakes but help guide them in making better decisions the next time around. Show kids how to network with other entrepreneurs or experienced business professionals for advice. Help kids develop an understanding of the risks and rewards associated with running a business. Finally, encourage them to think outside the box and be creative in coming up with unique business ideas. With the right guidance and dedication, any kid can become a millionaire!

How To Network With Other Entrepreneurs Or Experienced Business Professionals

Networking is an important part of becoming a successful entrepreneur. As a young person, it can be difficult to reach out and network with experienced business professionals or other entrepreneurs. However, several strategies can help kids create strong connections in the professional world.

One way to start networking as a kid is by attending conferences and events related to entrepreneurship and business. These events are great opportunities to meet other entrepreneurs and experienced business professionals in the industry. It is important to be prepared with questions and have an understanding of the topics being discussed so that you can make a good impression.

Another way to network is through online communities or forums related to entrepreneurship. Participating in these conversations allows kids to connect with people who share similar interests and learn from their experiences. You could also join a professional organization in your area that is focused on mentorship and networking, such as the Young Entrepreneurs Council or Junior Achievement.

Finally, don't forget to make use of social media! Reach out to entrepreneurs and business professionals you admire online and show interest in what they do. Following them on Twitter, Instagram, or LinkedIn can be a great way to start conversations and build relations

Risks And Rewards Associated With Running A Business

Risks and rewards associated with running a business should be discussed with kids when encouraging entrepreneurial opportunities. It's important to tell them that while running a business carries potential risks, it also presents the possibility of great rewards. By instilling an understanding of both, they will be better equipped to make informed decisions as they pursue their career goals. Additionally, teaching children about budgeting and setting up financial plans from a young age will also give them the necessary skills to effectively manage their business finances. By learning these essential money management principles, they can ensure that any risks associated with running a business are minimized and that their rewards are reaped. As such, it is important to make sure kids understand the challenges and benefits associated with entrepreneurship so they can develop the necessary skills to be successful in this field.

Identifying Opportunities

Identifying opportunities is one of the most important skills that can help kids become millionaires. Kids need to learn how to recognize potential opportunities and evaluate them before taking action. They should also consider what kind of risks are involved with pursuing a particular opportunity. Kids need to remember that not all opportunities will be successful, but this doesn't mean they shouldn't take chances. They should be able to recognize a good opportunity when it presents itself and be prepared to act on it quickly.

Kids can also identify opportunities in the business world. Whether it is starting a small business or investing in a larger one, kids need to develop an understanding of what it takes to be successful and create a business plan. They should also consider how they're going to market their product or service and what kind of resources will be required.

Finally, kids should learn how to network in order to identify potential opportunities. Networking is a great way for kids to meet people with similar interests and goals who can help them explore potential business or investment ideas. With the right resources and connections, kids can start to make their dreams of becoming a millionaire come true.

Overall, identifying opportunities is an essential skill for kids to learn if they want to become millionaires. They need to understand how the stock market works and how to evaluate potential investments before committing money. Kids should also consider starting or investing in a business and networking with the right people in order to get ahead. With the right knowledge and resources, kids can take advantage of opportunities they come across.

Millionaire Mindset

A millionaire mindset is the key to becoming successful as a young person. It's all about having an entrepreneurial attitude, setting goals, and taking action to achieve them. The first step towards achieving millionaire status is developing a self-belief that you can make it happen. This involves building confidence in yourself, believing that anything is possible with hard work and dedication. Next, you have to cultivate a positive attitude and take risks when necessary. Don't be afraid of failure or rejection. Instead, use it as motivation to try again and strive for success. Finally, focus on learning from your mistakes and making the most of every opportunity that comes your way.

Having a millionaire mindset means being proactive in order to make money work for you. This includes learning how to invest in yourself, your ideas, and the stock market. It also involves researching new business opportunities and taking advantage of them when they arise.

Millionaire kids are a testament to the fact that anyone can rise to success with the right mindset. By believing in yourself, setting achievable goals, and taking calculated risks, you too can become a millionaire. All it takes is the right attitude and a little hard work. With dedication and perseverance, you'll be on your way to achieving financial freedom.

Self-Belief

self-belief is an essential part of becoming a millionaire kid. It serves as the foundation for success and helps to create the mindset of abundance that is often necessary for achieving financial wealth. Kids who believe in themselves are more likely to take risks, try new things, and find creative solutions that can lead to greater success. Self-belief also instils a sense of optimism, enabling them to see the potential for success even in difficult situations.

By teaching kids to believe in themselves and their own capabilities, parents can help them to become more confident and resilient in the face of life's challenges. They can be encouraged to focus on their strengths rather than their weaknesses, taking pride in accomplishments while learning from mistakes.

Parents should also encourage children to set achievable and realistic goals, helping them to visualize their desired outcomes. With a clear vision in mind, kids can take the necessary steps towards achieving those goals with confidence. At the same time, they should also be taught how to manage their money responsibly. This includes budgeting and setting aside money for investments that will help them to build wealth over time.

Confidence In Himself

confidence in himself is essential for a millionaire kid. He must believe in his own abilities and have faith that he can achieve whatever goal he sets. Building self-confidence begins with positive thinking and setting realistic goals. A millionaire kid should celebrate successes, both big and small, and not be afraid to take risks. Through these methods, the young entrepreneur will develop an unshakeable belief in himself and his own potential to achieve great things. It's also important for a millionaire kid to surround himself with positive, supportive people who believe in him and can help him build up self-esteem. Finally, young entrepreneurs should be persistent and never give up on their dreams or goals – they will only get richer when the going gets tough. With confidence in himself, a millionaire kid will be better equipped to take on the world and make his or her fortune.

Believing That Anything

Believing that anything is possible is one of the

main qualities of millionaire kids. There are many other ways to become a millionaire kid, such as setting goals, having a good attitude, and managing money wisely. Setting clear and achievable goals gives children something to strive towards; it also helps them stay motivated and focused. In addition, having a positive attitude can help children develop good habits for success in the future. Finally, effective money management skills are essential for any millionaire kid, and these can be learned from a young age. By developing these qualities at an early age, children can gradually become millionaires as they grow older. With determination and perseverance, anything is possible!

Self-Esteem

Self-Esteem is an essential factor to teach millionaire kids. Self-esteem is a person's beliefs and feelings about themselves and their ability to cope with the challenges of life. It affects how people think, feel, and behave in different situations. Teaching kids self-esteem helps to empower them as they learn skills for success, such as problem-solving, creating goals, taking risks, and developing relationships. Self-esteem is an important factor in helping millionaire kids develop a positive outlook on life and reach their goals.

Parents can help foster healthy self-esteem in their children by providing unconditional love and support, creating a safe environment for open communication, setting clear expectations and boundaries, listening to the needs of their children, and praising them for effort rather than results. It is also important to instil a sense of responsibility in children; teaching them the value of hard work, setting realistic goals, and helping them develop the skills needed to be successful. A healthy self-esteem can help millionaire kids achieve success by enabling them to stay motivated, take risks, and remain resilient when faced with adversity.

Taking time out for self-care is also important in building healthy self-esteem. Encouraging kids to spend time outdoors, take part in activities that bring them joy, and set aside time for themselves can all help to foster a sense of well-being.

Manage Their Emotions

Millionaire kids need to be able to manage their emotions in order to maximize their success. This is especially important when they are dealing with money, as emotions can lead people to make irrational decisions.

One of the best ways for kids to start managing their emotions is through mindfulness—being aware of and accepting thoughts, feelings, and sensations without judgement or reacting. Practising mindfulness can help kids learn to observe and manage their emotions in a way that is more constructive than reactive.

It also helps kids to have an understanding of how different emotions affect them, so they can recognize when they are feeling overwhelmed or out of control and adjust accordingly. Teaching kids how to identify what they're feeling and take action in response can help them to become more emotionally resilient.

Other tips to help millionaire kids manage their emotions include having a support system of adults or peers that they can talk to when they're feeling overwhelmed, setting limits and boundaries for themselves regarding how much stress and pressure they put on themselves, and finding healthy activities such as exercise or creative hobbies that can be used as outlets for their emotions.

By teaching kids how to manage their emotions constructively, they can become more successful millionaires and better understand the challenges that come with handling money. This way, they will be well-prepared to make sound decisions for themselves and their futures.

Exercise

Exercise is another great way for millionaire kids to build their self-esteem. Exercise releases endorphins which can boost our mood and give us a sense of accomplishment. It can also provide an outlet for stress, helping us develop healthy coping strategies that aren't dependent on material gain or success. Exercising with friends or joining a team can also help improve social skills and build confidence in ourselves and our abilities. Finally, finding a physical activity that we enjoy can help us to stay motivated and engaged with the task of improving our self-esteem.

No matter how millionaire kids choose to exercise, they should be sure to set realistic goals that are achievable and tailored to their own fitness level. Becoming overwhelmed by expectations can take away from the fun and accomplishment of physical activity. Keeping a positive outlook and having significant others who are supportive can also help to keep them motivated and on track with their goals. With consistent effort, millionaire kids can build self-esteem through physical activity that will last for many years to come.

Mindfulness

Millionaire kids can benefit from developing mindfulness skills to help them navigate the unique challenges they face. Mindfulness is a state of being where one is aware and present at the moment, without judgment or expectations. It helps people recognize their thoughts and feelings, as well as observe those experiences rather than reacting to them impulsively. For young millionaires especially, it can be useful for developing healthy coping strategies and managing difficult emotions.

Mindfulness activities can include breathing exercises, meditation, mindful self-care, or yoga. When practised regularly, these activities can help kids become more aware of their thoughts and feelings which can lead to improved self-esteem. Additionally, mindfulness helps children better understand themselves and how they relate to the world around them, which can ultimately contribute to a healthier sense of self-worth.

Ultimately, developing healthy habits and fostering positive self-esteem is key to building resilience in millionaire kids. By incorporating mindfulness into their lives, children can create the strong foundation they need to cope with the unique pressures and challenges they face.

Relaxation Techniques

Relaxation techniques are an important tool for millionaire kids in managing their stress. Taking regular breaks throughout the day, deep breathing exercises, and progressive muscle relaxation can help reduce the effects of daily stress.

When faced with a stressful situation, it's important to remember that taking care of oneself is just as important as taking care of business matters. Healthy coping strategies such as yoga, meditation, and mindful journaling can help millionaire kids stay grounded and focused on their goals.

In addition to relaxation techniques, millionaire kids need to incorporate physical activity into their daily routines. Taking walks outside in the fresh air or engaging in a favourite sport can help clear the mind and reduce stress levels. Regular physical activity also helps enhance creativity and productivity, both of which are essential for attaining financial success.

In order to become a millionaire kid, it's important to learn how to manage stress and make healthy lifestyle choices. Relaxation techniques, physical activity, and mindful practices can help reduce the effects of daily stress while also enhancing creativity and productivity. By incorporating these strategies into one's routine, millionaire kids can achieve their goals while also maintaining a healthy lifestyle.

Lessons Learned From Their Experiences

Lessons learned from their experiences of becoming millionaires as kids can be applied by anyone, regardless of age. One key lesson is to never give up on a dream. No matter how difficult it may seem, stay focused and keep working hard towards achieving the goal. Additionally, many kid millionaires learned to think outside the box and come up with creative solutions for problems or situations they encounter. They also understood that sometimes taking a risk and investing in themselves can be incredibly rewarding. Additionally, they cultivated strong relationships with mentors and other successful people who could offer advice, support and guidance along the way. Finally, these young millionaires embraced failure as part of the process -- it is important to learn from mistakes, grow from them, and use those experiences to reach success. By taking all of these lessons into consideration, anyone can become a millionaire.

If you want to be a millionaire as a kid, it is important to remember the lessons learned from their experiences and use them to your advantage. With hard work, dedication, creativity, risk-taking and resilience, you can make your dreams a reality. It is all about taking the first step in the right direction.

Learning New Skills

Learning New Skills is an essential part of the path to becoming a millionaire kid. By expanding their knowledge and developing existing skills, kids can open more doors of opportunities available to them. They can learn new ideas and concepts that will help them in their journey, whether it be starting a business or investing in stocks.

There are many ways for kids to learn new skills, such as attending courses, workshops and seminars. They can also read books, watch instructional videos or podcasts, and attend apprenticeships. These activities can help them to acquire the basic skills needed to be successful in their chosen field.

Additionally, kids need to stay up-to-date with current trends in their industry by reading articles and blogs related to their topics of interest. This will help them to stay abreast of the latest developments and gain insights from industry experts. They should also take advantage of online courses that offer interactive tutorials and challenging assignments, which can give them greater knowledge and understanding of various topics related to their field.

Attending Courses

Attending courses is one of the most effective ways to become a millionaire kid. From online courses to traditional college classes, there are plenty of opportunities for kids to learn new skills that will help them succeed in business and life. With an array of options available, kids need to find the right course that will truly benefit their goals.

For example, attending a course on entrepreneurship can provide kids with the valuable knowledge and skills needed to start their own businesses. There are also courses available in financial literacy, which can help kids learn how to manage money better and save for a more secure future. Additionally, attending classes in areas such as coding or graphic design will give children the tools they need to launch successful businesses by creating digital products or services.

By attending the right courses, kids can build a strong foundation of knowledge that will help them reach their goals and become a millionaire. Furthermore, it's important to remember that business success is not just about having the necessary skills, but also building relationships with mentors and other people who are working in similar fields. Attending courses can therefore provide an opportunity to network and start building the relationships necessary for success.

The bottom line is that attending courses can be a great way for kids to learn new skills and gain knowledge that will help them become millionaires. With the right course, kids can make sure they're getting the most out of their learning experience and setting themselves up for success in the future. It's never too early to start investing in knowledge, and attending courses is the perfect way for kids to get started.

Workshops

workshops are a great way for kids to learn new skills and build upon existing ones. They provide an opportunity for hands-on learning in a structured environment with experienced instructors who can guide your child through the entire process of mastering something new. Taking part in workshops gives kids the chance to gain valuable knowledge, develop their problem-solving capabilities, and even increase their confidence. It's also a great way for them to make new friends and get out of their comfort zone. With the right workshops, kids can find themselves on the path to becoming millionaires by mastering skills that help them succeed in life. From coding and robotics to finance and business, there's no limit to what your child can learn at a workshop. So, don't hesitate to enroll your kid in one today and help them get started on their path to becoming a millionaire. By learning new skills, they'll be well-equipped to handle any challenge that comes their way.

Seminars

One way for kids to become millionaires is by attending seminars. Seminars can provide children with the opportunity to learn new skills and gain valuable knowledge that will help them in their future endeavours. Attending seminars allows children to network and build relationships with professionals in their field of interest, as well as other entrepreneurs. It also gives them a chance to ask questions and get advice from experienced businesspeople. Seminars are a great way for kids to gain knowledge and insights that will help them become successful entrepreneurs and millionaires. Additionally, these seminars often provide resources such as books, videos, or documents that can further educate the child on topics related to their chosen field of study. By attending seminars, children can gain the skills they need to become a success in any field they choose.

Additionally, seminars can be a great way to meet like-minded people and create relationships with professionals. These relationships can be helpful in the future when seeking advice or resources related to their business endeavours. By attending seminars, children can make connections with people who are already successful and learn from their experiences. This can help kids become millionaires faster as they have the resources and knowledge to make informed business decisions.

Problem-Solving Skill

problem-solving Skill is one of the essential skills for

kids to become millionaires. Children who possess such skills are able to identify, analyze and resolve difficult problems more effectively than their peers. Teaching these problem-solving Skills will help kids develop strong decision-making abilities which are necessary to become successful in life.

In order to foster problem-solving skills in children, parents can encourage them to think critically about potential solutions. Additionally, parents can provide their kids with challenging tasks and problems that require them to apply their problem-solving Skills. This can include activities such as puzzles, board games, science experiments and other activities that require creative thinking and logical reasoning.

Parents should also model problem-solving behaviours in the home environment, so that they can demonstrate to their children how to effectively tackle problems. This could involve encouraging kids to think of multiple solutions and considering the pros and cons of each option before making a decision.

Finally, parents need to provide their children with the necessary resources in order to help them develop their problem-solving Skills. This may include books on problem-solving strategies, providing access to problem-solving software or enrolling them in extracurricular activities that focus on problem-solving Skills.

Communication Skills

Communication Skills are an essential part of becoming a millionaire kid. Kids need to learn how to communicate effectively with others and develop their own communication styles. Communication skills allow kids to express themselves clearly and concisely in any situation. This includes presenting ideas, giving feedback, asking questions, and resolving conflicts.

When it comes to communicating with others, millionaire kids should strive to be good listener. It is important for them to actively listen and understand what others are saying before they respond. This can help them build relationships, as well as strengthen their own ideas.

Millionaire kids should also practice active speaking skills by learning how to form complete sentences and ask meaningful questions. They should learn how to be clear and concise when presenting their ideas, as well as how to use persuasive language in order to influence others.

Millionaire kids should strive to stay calm and in control of their emotions during conversations. This will help them remain effective when dealing with difficult conversations, as well as any conflicts that may arise. It is important for kids to learn how to stay composed during any sort of conversation, and to use their communication skills in order to effectively resolve conflicts.

Decision-Making Skills

Decision-making Skills are essential for millionaire

kids. These skills can be developed by teaching children how to think critically and weigh the consequences of their decisions. When making decisions, they should also consider the long-term effects on their financial well-being.

Parents can help their children become better decision-makers by encouraging them to ask questions and do research before making any choices. They can also provide guidance and offer advice on how to deal with difficult situations. Children need to understand that there may be consequences when they make poor decisions and that these consequences can have a lasting impact on their financial future.

Children should also learn how to weigh the costs and benefits of each decision before making it. They should take into account the potential risks as well as the potential rewards. This will help them make better decisions in the long run and become more confident in their own decision-making abilities.

When making any important financial decisions, it is also important for children to seek advice from those who are knowledgeable and experienced in the field. By doing so, they can gain valuable insight into how to best manage their money and make better financial decisions.

Finally, children should also be taught the importance of patience and discipline when making decisions. By taking the time to properly consider their options and consequences, they can ensure that their decisions are sound and beneficial in the long run. With these decision-making skills, millionaire kids will have a greater chance of success as they grow older.

Organization Skills

Organization Skills are key for any aspiring millionaire kid. With the right skills, kids can learn how to stay organized and plan to make sure their goals are achieved.

Organization Skills begin with basic time management techniques such as daily planning, lists, reminders, and tracking progress. Kids should create a schedule that works for them to ensure they have enough time for schoolwork and other activities. When it comes to lists, kids should separate tasks according to priority and timeline. For example, they can create a "To Do" list for things that need to be done right away and a "Future To-Do" list for any tasks they want to complete in the future. Keeping track of progress is also important for staying motivated and knowing when goals are reached.

In addition to time management, organization skills also include being able to sort through information and prioritize tasks. Kids should be encouraged to filter out any unnecessary information that might distract them from reaching their goals. They should also learn how to break large tasks down into smaller steps in order to make them more manageable.

Supporting The Community

Supporting The Community is an important part of how to become millionaire kids. It can be done in a variety of ways, such as donating money or resources to local charities, volunteering with community events and organizations, or even simply helping out neighbours in need. Giving back to the community can not only help those in need but also show young people that they can make an impact.

Another way for millionaire kids to give back is by mentoring a younger generation. Becoming a mentor not only helps young people learn about skills and values, but it also shows them the importance of passing on knowledge and giving back. With the right guidance, these children can become leaders within their own communities and help those in need through volunteering or fundraising initiatives.

Finally, millionaire kids can also get involved in local politics and help bring positive changes to their communities. By getting involved in issues, they can learn how important it is to be an active member of the community and how to make a difference. Whether it's by attending town hall meetings or running for office, young people have a chance to shape the future of their communities and make a real impact.

Supporting the community is an important part of how to become millionaire kids, as it can lead to a greater sense of purpose and build character. By giving back, young people will gain valuable skills and life lessons that will help them in both their personal lives and future careers. With the right guidance and determination, millionaire kids can make an impact in their local communities and become a positive example for others to follow.

Real-Life Examples And Success Stories Of Millionaire Kids

Real-life examples and success stories of millionaire kids can provide valuable insights into how young people have achieved success and financial independence. Some of the most successful millionaire kids include Mark Zuckerberg, who became a billionaire after founding Facebook, and Evan Spiegel, the co-founder of Snapchat. These entrepreneurs started their businesses at an early age and used innovative technologies to become millionaires by their mid-twenties.

Other examples of millionaire kids include YouTube star Cameron Dallas, who earned millions from his videos and other social media endorsements; Ashton Kutcher, an actor and investor who co-founded venture capital firm A-Grade Investments; and Shawn Fanning, the creator of Napster. These individuals achieved success through hard work, perseverance, and dedication to their respective fields.

These examples demonstrate that the journey to becoming a millionaire is an attainable goal, no matter how young you are. With the right strategy and dedication, it's possible to achieve financial success at any age. It's important to remember that these millionaires didn't just rely on luck – they worked hard to get where they are today. If you have a dream of one day becoming a millionaire, you should look to these success stories for inspiration and guidance. With the right attitude, dedication, and strategy, it's possible to make your dreams a reality.

CHAPTER 6: TIPS AND TRICKS FOR PARENTS

1\. Encourage your child to take risks and be entrepreneurial from a young age
1. Provide them with educational resources that focus on money management, business principles, investment strategies, and more. This will help them understand how important it is to have a good knowledge of financial matters for success in life.
2. Offer support and guidance but don't be too controlling. Let them make some mistakes, learn from them and become more self-reliant.
3. Encourage risk-taking by providing a safe environment to practice it in their daily life. It can be as simple as allowing your child to try different types of activities or experiences that they would normally not think of doing.
4. Teach them to think critically and be creative. As they develop skills, introduce them to different business ideas and the process of planning and launching their own enterprise.
5. Celebrate successes, no matter how small they may seem. This will help motivate them to keep going, even when things get tough.
6. Show your child that failure is an inevitable part of success. Remind them that even the biggest and most successful people have faced failure, but they

got back up and kept going no matter what.

7. Provide your child with mentors who can help them understand their own motivations and goals and provide advice on how to achieve these objectives.

8. Make sure to take a long-term approach, focusing on building skills and financial knowledge rather than short-term gains.

9. Encourage your child to save a portion of their earnings for future investments, so they can realize the power of compound interest.

10. Finally, instil in them the idea that money is not an end goal but a tool to help them reach their dreams and goals in life. This will provide them with the motivation to consistently work hard and reach their full potential.

2. Set Clear Expectations Early On Regarding Money And Hard Work

Parents should set expectations early on about money and hard work in order to help their children become millionaires. Teaching kids the value of hard work, discipline, and financial responsibility from an early age will pay dividends down the road. The best way for parents to start teaching these values is by setting clear expectations around money and how it's earned.

First, it's important to discuss how money is earned and what hard work involves. Explain to kids that in order to earn money, they must put forth effort and dedication. Show them examples of people who have worked hard and achieved success. It's also beneficial for parents to lead by example and show their children what hard work looks like.

Second, parents should emphasize the importance of saving. Kids should understand that money isn't simply for spending and that it must be set aside in order to build up savings or investments. Show them how their money can generate income with interest or dividends over time.

Third, it's important to teach kids about budgeting. Explain how they need to think about how much money they have and how it should be allocated. Show them how to track their expenses and create a budget that focuses on saving, short-term goals, and long-term investments.

Finally, parents should teach kids the basics of investing. Explain the different types of investment accounts: stocks, bonds, mutual funds, etc., as well as the concepts of risk and reward. Once kids understand the basics, they can start to think about investing in specific stocks or funds that match their goals and risk tolerance.

By setting clear expectations early on about money and hard work, parents can help their children become millionaires. With discipline, dedication, and wise investments, children will be well on their way to financial success.

3. Encourage Your Child's Dreams But Also Show Them How Their Talents Can Be Used To Make Money In The Long Run

The key to helping your child become a millionaire is to foster their dreams and help them explore how they can turn their talents into profitable ventures. Start by having conversations with your kid about what they love to do, then encourage them to think of ways they could monetize the activity. If your child loves sports, for instance, suggest that they look into coaching younger kids or starting a sports camp. If your child loves writing, explore ways in which they can use their skills to write about topics for businesses or start a blog where they could monetize posts.

You should also help your kid think of other ways to make money through investments and business ventures. Research online resources that teach children how to become savvy investors and discuss with them the importance of smart spending and saving. You can help them open a savings account and teach them the basics of budgeting. Consider giving your child an allowance that they can use to invest in stocks or small business opportunities like selling handmade items online.

4. Guide Your Child In Understanding The Importance Of Having Multiple Sources Of Income, And How To Make Their Money Work For Them

Parents can help their children become millionaires by teaching them the importance of having multiple sources of income. Encourage your child to look for ways to generate extra income such as getting a part-time job, starting a business or investing in stocks or real estate. Explain that these strategies will help them build up wealth over time and provide an additional stream of income.

In addition to having multiple sources of income, children need to understand how to make their money work for them. Teach your child the basics of investing and show them how they can use stocks, bonds, mutual funds and other investments to grow their wealth over time. Explain that these long-term investments will help ensure financial security in the future.

Encourage your child to use the money they make from their various sources of income to create a budget and set financial goals. Teach them the importance of living within their means and saving for the future. Explain that by creating a budget and setting financial goals, they will be able to better manage their money and use it more efficiently to reach their long-term financial goals.

Finally, it's important to teach your child the importance of taking risks and taking advantage of opportunities when they arise. Explain that by being bold and taking calculated risks, they could potentially reap significant rewards in the future. Encourage them to think outside the box and come up with creative ideas on how to make their money work for them.

5. Help Your Children Identify Mentors Who Can Help Them To Grow Professionally And Personally

One of the best ways to help your children become millionaires is to encourage them to find mentors who can help guide their way. Mentors are experienced professionals in their field and can provide invaluable guidance to young aspiring entrepreneurs. They should have a strong track record of success in their field, be passionate about what they do, and be willing to listen and offer advice.

Encourage your kids to start networking with professionals in their chosen fields. This could include attending professional conferences, joining industry-related forums or associations, and talking to people who have achieved success in the same area. Ask them to invite experienced mentors out for coffee or a chat – even if it's just over email or Skype.

You can also set up an online profile for your kids on a professional network such as LinkedIn. This will help them to build connections with potential mentors, and give them access to industry resources and trends that they wouldn't otherwise be able to find.

By having strong mentor relationships, your children can learn from the wisdom of experienced professionals and gain the confidence they need to become successful in their field. They'll also be able to get advice from mentors on how to make the most of their money, such as investments and other strategies that can help them build wealth over time.

Help your children find mentors who will be genuinely invested in their success – not only financially but emotionally too. With the right support network of knowledgeable professionals, your kids can be well on their way to becoming millionaires.

6. Encourage Your Children To Explore Different Fields, So They Get A Better Understanding Of The Job Market And Their Options For Wealth Creation

The best way to help kids become millionaires is to get them interested in the world of business and entrepreneurship. The earlier they start exploring different fields, the better it will be for their future. Parents can encourage this curiosity by teaching their children about different industries, encouraging them to attend industry events or seminars, providing resources about successful entrepreneurs, and finding mentors who can guide them in their journey.

Another important step for parents is to encourage their children to try out different job options. By exploring the job market, kids can gain an understanding of what careers offer higher earning potential and the skills required to succeed in those fields. This will help them make better-informed decisions when pursuing a career that could potentially lead them towards financial freedom.

Finally, parents should also take the time to teach their kids how to invest and save money. They need to understand that having a good financial plan is essential in order to achieve long-term success. Additionally, teaching kids about the importance of budgeting can help them manage their expenses while still allowing them to make smart investments with their money. All of these steps can eventually lead them to create wealth and become millionaires in the future.

By providing their children with the right knowledge and access to resources, parents can help kids learn how to create wealth and set themselves up for long-term success. By taking these steps, kids will be better prepared to enter the job market and make the most out of their earning potential.

7. Show Your Kids How Hard Work Pays Off And The Importance Of Dedication And Consistency In Order To Achieve Their Goals

One of the most important lessons you can teach your kids is about the power of hard work and dedication. Showing them how their consistent efforts can lead to success will demonstrate to them that they have control over their future. Here are some tips on showing your kids how hard work pays off:

- Lead by example. Set a good example for your children by working hard yourself and demonstrating how that effort leads to success.

- Celebrate their efforts. Whenever your child puts in extra work, make sure to recognize it and celebrate their achievements. This will help them understand the value of hard work and motivate them to keep pushing forward.
- Talk about the importance of dedication and consistency. Explain why dedication and consistency are so important in achieving goals. Show them how hard work over time can result in success, and teach them that sometimes failure is part of the journey.
- Show them the reward. Explain to your kids that when they put in the effort they will be rewarded with positive outcomes. Demonstrate this by showing them tangible results from their hard work like improved grades or a better job.

8. Let Your Children Make Mistakes, It's Part Of Learning From Them For Future Success

Teaching children the right lessons in life is a crucial part of forming their future success. One important lesson for kids is to learn from making mistakes and take responsibility for them. Parents should encourage their children to make mistakes, so long as it's within reasonable limits and won't cause any serious harm. Making mistakes helps children identify the consequences of their actions, develop problem-solving skills, and learn how to take responsibility for their mistakes.

It can be hard for parents to watch their children make mistakes, but it is an important part of helping them in the long run. It's important to stay calm and explain why the mistake happened so your child can understand what they could do differently next time. Instead of using the 'fear factor' to prevent your children from making mistakes, encourage them to learn from it and make better decisions in the future.

For example, if your child fails a test or an assignment at school, let them experience the consequences of their actions and help them reflect on what could have been done differently. Talk through possible solutions with them so they can understand how changing their approach could lead to different results. Encourage them to take ownership of the situation and come up with new strategies for improving in the future.

By letting your children make mistakes, it's part of learning from them for future success. Valuable lessons such as resilience, problem-solving, and taking responsibility are all essential skills that will help your child become a millionaire in the future. It's up to parents to provide guidance and support when their children make mistakes, so that they can learn from them and take ownership of their decisions.

9. Make Sure You Teach Your Children The Importance Of Giving Back And Helping Others, So They Learn To Be Generous With Their Riches

Having financial success doesn't just mean having wealth and living a comfortable life. It also means using your resources to build a better future, both for yourself and those around you.

Teaching children the importance of helping others is an important part of showing them how to be responsible with their money. Encourage kids to donate time, money or goods to charity. Explain why it's important to give back and make sure they understand how their generosity can help others.

Also, if you have money to spare, think of other ways your family can use it for the greater good. You could invest in a business or organization that is focused on sustainable development or social responsibility. Or set up scholarships or grants for students in need. By teaching your children to be generous with their wealth, you will help them develop a sense of responsibility and appreciation for their financial success. In addition, they will learn that money can be used for more than just buying material things; it can also be used to make the world a better place.

10. Help Your Children Understand How To Network And Build Relationships Which Can Help Them In The Long Run?

As parents, one of the best ways to help our children become millionaires is to equip them with the knowledge and skills needed to network successfully. Networking is one of the essential elements for achieving success in any field, so it's important to teach your kids how to make meaningful connections and nurture relationships. Start by teaching your children about basic social etiquette such as introducing themselves and being polite. Encourage them to make conversation with people they meet, ask questions, and actually listen to the answers. Show them how they can use these conversations to learn more about their peers and build relationships which could lead to valuable opportunities down the road.

Help your children understand the importance of networking by introducing them to individuals in your own network. Encourage them to attend networking events, such as seminars or conferences, and show them how to properly introduce themselves and make meaningful conversations.

It's also important to teach your children the importance of maintaining these relationships. Show them how they can stay in touch with individuals they meet, by sending a quick message or calling every once in a while. Explain that these connections can be beneficial in the future and highlight successful networking stories of your own.

By equipping your children with the knowledge and skills needed to network successfully, you'll help them build valuable relationships which could lead to great opportunities in the future – something that will benefit them immensely throughout their lives.

How To Set An Example If You Are Millionaire Parent

For millionaire parents, setting an example is

essential to teaching their kids about the importance of hard work and smart money management. These children need to understand that wealth comes from the consistent application of good habits, not just luck or inheritance. Here are some tips on how millionaire parents can set a positive example for their children.

1. Demonstrate a positive attitude: Millionaire parents should strive to show their kids that having a positive outlook and strong work ethic is the key to success, both personally and financially. Doing so will help instil these same values in your children.

2. Speak openly about money management: Millionaire parents should talk to their children about money management and how it can affect their lives. Make sure your kids understand the importance of budgeting, saving, and investing wisely in order to continue growing wealth over time.

3. Show your kids that hard work pays off: Millionaire parents should demonstrate that success comes from dedication and hard work by always putting in the extra effort and staying motivated. Show your kids that working hard for what you want pays off, and it's worth every bit of effort.

4. Encourage financial literacy: Having a basic understanding of personal finance is essential for success in today's world. Make sure your kids understand the basics of budgeting, investing, debt management and more.

5. Support their dreams: Show your kids that you

believe in them by supporting their passions and encouraging them to pursue their dreams. This will help instil a sense of confidence and pride in your children, teaching them that they are capable of achieving great things.

Stay Positive

Staying positive is a key component to becoming a millionaire kid. It can be hard to stay optimistic when the going gets tough, but you mustn't lose sight of your end goal. Having a positive attitude will help keep you motivated and focused on achieving success. Take the time to recognize and celebrate even small successes, no matter how insignificant they may seem. This will help you stay motivated and remind yourself that you are on the right track. When there are setbacks, instead of getting discouraged, use it as an opportunity to learn and grow from the experience. Additionally, staying positive can have a domino effect - if you remain positive, those around will also feel more optimistic which can lead to success for everyone. So, stay positive and don't be afraid to take risks - it could be the key to achieving your dreams of becoming a millionaire kid.

CONCLUSION

How to millionaire kids is a program designed to teach children the fundamentals of financial literacy and how to become financially independent. It is divided into four parts: understanding money, budgeting, investing, and building wealth.

In the first part, children learn about the different forms of money such as cash, credit cards, checks and debit cards. They also learn about the basics of inflation, exchange rates, and interest. This knowledge helps them understand how money works in their everyday lives.

Next, children learn about budgeting and creating a spending plan. They also learn about saving for short-term goals and long-term goals such as college tuition or retirement.

In the third part, children learn about investing. This includes understanding the stock market, mutual funds, and other investment vehicles. They also learn about risk management and diversification.

Children learn how to build wealth. This involves setting up a portfolio of investments that can generate passive income over time such as real estate or business ownership. They also learn about taxes and legal strategies to help protect their wealth.

The best way for young kids to learn financial responsibility is by setting financial goals. For children ages six to eight, the goals should be simple and achievable. They must understand why these goals are important so that they feel motivated and inspired as they work towards achieving them. Here are some ideas for setting financial goals:

- Introduce your child to the concept of saving money. Start by encouraging them to put aside some of their allowance or gifts for a rainy day fund. Make sure they understand that this is not an opportunity to spend, but rather a way to build up money for later use.

- Teach your child how to budget and track their finances. Show them how to use a program such as Mint, or a simple spreadsheet, to track and record expenses. Help them understand why it's important to set financial goals and track spending.

- Introduce your child to different types of investments and saving options. Help them understand what they are investing in and the risks associated with various investments. Explain why it's important to diversify their portfolio and the different ways that money can grow over time.

- Encourage your child to use their extra money for charitable giving or other causes. This will help them learn the importance of giving back to their community, as well as how to make wise spending decisions with their finances.

why cultivating strong financial habits early in childhood matters:

1. Learning the value of money: Teaching kids the importance of saving can help them learn how to

budget and better manage their finances. Setting up a savings account or teaching kids about the stock market can also give them an understanding of how to make their money work for them in the future.

2. Developing smart spending habits: Kids should learn from a young age that money is a limited resource, and they should be mindful of how they use it. Encouraging kids to think about the long-term value of their purchases will help them make better decisions now and in the future.

3. Building financial confidence: Teaching kids about basic financial topics such as budgeting, saving, and investing can help them develop a sense of financial confidence. Having this type of knowledge can give kids the tools and resources to make sound financial decisions and potentially become millionaires in the future.

4. Avoiding costly mistakes: Teaching kids about money early on can help them avoid making expensive financial mistakes in the future. Helping children understand the consequences of poor financial decisions, such as overspending or taking on too much debt, can put them in a better position to manage their finances responsibly when they become adults.

MAY I ASK YOU FOR A SMALL FAVOR?

Before you go, please I need your assistance! In case you like this book, might you be able to please share your opinion on Amazon and compose a legit review? It will take only one moment for you, yet be an extraordinary favour for me. Since I'm not a famous writer and I don't have a large distributing organization supporting me. I read each and every review and hop around with happiness like a little child each time my audience remark on my books and gives me their fair criticism! ☺. In case you didn't appreciate the book or had an issue with it, kindly get in touch with me via my email; Adamdiesel@gmail.com and reveal to me how I can improve it.

Made in the USA
Las Vegas, NV
10 December 2023